PRAISE FOR

# Before you Live together

My friend Dave Gudgel has written a very sensible and
sensitive book on a very important issue. You should read it
for yourself and then get a copy for every couple you care about that
is considering living together without getting married.
This well-researched and commonsense book could save a lot
of heartache. I highly recommend it.

### DR. NEIL T. ANDERSON
FREEDOM IN CHRIST MINISTRIES

Dave Gudgel offers some thought-provoking, humorous
and biblical reasons to follow God's blueprint for a romantic
relationship. If couples want to do marriage right and
make it last, they would do well to read
*Before You Live Together* as soon as possible.

### KIRK CAMERON
ACTOR

"I wouldn't buy a car without driving it, so taking my potential mate for a test drive only makes good sense." This sounds like a logical conclusion until you understand that our ways are not God's ways. My friend Dave Gudgel unwinds the logic of living together before marriage, establishes how harmful it is to the couple and to society and then shows a better way.

My daddy was a bookie. Being raised as a gambler's kid, I understand odds. I know not to bet very much on a long shot. Dave shows how living together before marriage makes a successful marriage a long shot at best. This book is a must-read for people of all ages who are seriously dating and for those who have already put their future marriage at risk.

### JAY CARTY
YES! MINISTRIES

Wisdom begins with understanding the wisdom of God in our lives. *Before You Live Together* gives you a taste of how wise God is. This is a must-read for those who desire God's blessing upon their marriage.

### DR. DARRYL DELHOUSAYE
SENIOR PASTOR, SCOTTSDALE BIBLE CHURCH
PRESIDENT, PHOENIX SEMINARY

With thought-provoking insight, Dave Gudgel has crafted an excellent resource for anyone who is involved in counseling young couples. I appreciate his honesty and attention to carefully gathered statistics. *Before You Live Together* is a very helpful book!

### ROBIN JONES GUNN
BEST-SELLING AUTHOR, THE CHRISTY MILLER SERIES FOR TEENS AND THE GLENBROOKE SERIES

*Before You Live Together* is an important, practical and easy-to-read book. It is a valuable tool for those who are taking an honest look at marriage. By evaluating the pros and cons of living together before marriage, the book challenges current social trends and guides couples toward God's standards for happiness in relationships.

## BOB PHILLIPS
AUTHOR, COUNSELOR
DIRECTOR AT LARGE, HUME LAKE CHRISTIAN CAMPS

This book is long overdue. *Before You Live Together* deals with the cornerstone of a successful Christian marriage.
I recommend it without reservation.

## DR. KEN POURE
DIRECTOR EMERITUS, HUME LAKE CHRISTIAN CAMPS

If you're holding this book because a friend gave it to you, you can count that person as an exceptional friend. If you just picked it up, you can count yourself very wise for buying it and poring through its pages. From my perspective, *Before You Live Together* is a book that those of us in the counseling field have needed for years. From your perspective, it will give you the wisdom and sound counsel you will need to answer the hard questions on whether living together really works and makes sense. Before you make the decision to live together, read this book.

## JOHN TRENT, PH.D.
AUTHOR, SPEAKER
PRESIDENT, STRONGFAMILIES.COM

Dave Gudgel's book is packed with timely wisdom and warm encouragement. If you're contemplating a life together or if you counsel couples who are, you'll find life-changing insights in these pages. I highly recommend *Before You Live Together*.

BRUCE WILKINSON
AUTHOR, *NEW YORK TIMES* BEST-SELLERS
*THE PRAYER OF JABEZ* AND *A LIFE GOD REWARDS*

# Before you Live together

DAVID GUDGEL

Revell

a division of Baker Publishing Group
Grand Rapids, Michigan

Published by Revell
a division of Baker Publishing Group
PO Box 6287, Grand Rapids, MI 49516-6287
www.revellbooks.com

Revell edition published 2014
ISBN 978-0-8007-2523-5

Previously published by Regal Books

Printed in the United States of America

The Library of Congress has cataloged the previous edition as follows:
    Gudgel, David R.
      Before you live together / David Gudgel.
          p.  cm.
      Includes bibliographical references.
      ISBN 0-8307-3252-7
      1.  Unmarried couples—Religious aspects—Christianity. 2.
    Marriage—Religious aspects—Christianity. I. Title.
    BT705.9.G83 2003
    241′.66—dc21                                                        2003006583

The names of the couples whose stories are told in this book have been changed, but the illustrations are true.

Cover and interior design by Robert Williams
Edited by Steven Lawson

# Contents

# Part 2: How to Be Sure

# Part 3: Spiritual Insight

# ACKNOWLEDGMENTS

Writing this book has been a God-thing. I could not have done it without Him, nor could I have finished it without the people He put into my life who have helped me in innumerable ways:

Bernice—This book is as much your work as mine. I love you. I will get your list done. Promise.

Kyle—Thanks for believing that this book has great potential and for steering me in the right direction.

Steve—I asked for a good editor and I got the best. Thanks for your insights and amazing skill.

Frank and Carol—Thank you for opening up your pool house overlooking the golf course to me. It provided a perfect retreat for writing. I owe you BIG.

Rick, Dave, Dana, Steve and Dale—Your support, encouragement and insights helped immensely. I miss our support group.

Penny, Kathy, Nancy, Brent and Christine—Your initial editing and insights were worth it. It is finally published!

All my friends and extended church family at Agoura Bible Fellowship—You supported us and made it possible for me to write this book while I was between churches.

And to all of you who gave me permission to tell your stories—Pray with me that your openness and honesty will help others who are struggling with the same decision with which you have struggled and made.

# tHiNKiNG aBOUt moving in togetHeR?

In the 1970s a controversial television sitcom became a hit. *Three's Company* was the story of three single young adults—two women and one man—who decided to live together. Although their relationship was only platonic, the very thought of people of the opposite sex *who weren't married* cohabiting pushed the envelope of acceptable TV viewing.

Until the mid-twentieth century (*i.e.*, for thousands of years), the family unit had been the center of society: It consisted of a mom, a dad and the children. Normally a child lived with his or her parents until he or she was old enough—often between 16 and 20 years old—to get married and move into his or her own home with his or her spouse.

Society has changed a lot. As people choose to marry and start their families much later in life than their predecessors did, most young people end up living on their own for a while. Single adults have many options: They can stay in their parents' house, have their own apartment, share a home with friends of the same sex, move in with a group of men and women who are platonic friends or cohabit with someone with whom they are involved romantically. This book is focused on the latter group: two people who are dating and are considering living together before they get married.

Today, one out of two couples cohabit before they say "I do." Most who cohabit think they will get married—someday. But, for various reasons, they believe that it makes sense to live together first.

Even though there is no until-death-do-us-part commitment, living together before marriage is still a huge step. This big decision will impact the rest of their lives: regardless of whether they marry, they will never be the same. Unfortunately, most couples do not take the time to research whether they are sure they should live together to find out whether they are sure about marriage.

In this book I have compiled information that I hope will help people make wise decisions in this area. Perhaps you are thinking about living with someone. You could be at the point in a relationship where you are considering marriage. Maybe you have a friend or family member who is struggling with this decision. Possibly you are already living with someone you hope to one day marry. Or it could be that you are living with someone you never plan to marry.

Whichever the circumstances of your life, I hope to help you sort through your feelings and the myriad opinions about what is best for you: living together before getting married, or getting married and then living together.

# P A R T    1

# LIVING together

# IN THE BEGINNING

After college, Justin moved from Southern California to Washington, D.C., to follow a dream. His desire to enter the world of politics took him across the country to the center of where it all happens. He got a job working for his senator. Justin was the person you would talk to on the phone when you wanted tickets for a tour of the White House, the Capitol or any other popular spot.

Brooke was also interested in politics. She moved to D.C. from Ohio and began working for her congressman. She had the same job as Justin—dealing with myriad phone calls from constituents who desperately wanted tickets.

An unofficial e-mail system exists in D.C. that allows all of the people with this job to send messages to each other, offering to trade tickets for various tours. Because each person receives a lot of these e-mails each day, Justin decided to spice his up a bit, so people would be inclined to open his first. He started adding jokes and interesting bits of information. It worked. Before long, his e-mail messages became must-reads. He became somewhat of a legend within the system.

One night after work, Justin and some friends went to a bar. While there, a mutual friend introduced him to Brooke. When she heard his name, Brooke exclaimed, "Hey, you're the Justin Clark who sends those funny e-mails!"

With satisfaction, Justin thought, *Well this is absolutely wonderful. I don't even know this person, but she knows me. I love this reaction.* Justin and Brooke began a friendship that led to dating.

Feeling that he was not growing politically or professionally after four years in D.C., Justin decided to move back to his hometown and run for city council. He felt this move would help him get closer to achieving his dream of actually *being* a politician instead of just answering a politician's phone.

Brooke was also ready for a change. They had been dating for a while, and when Justin asked her if she wanted to go with him, she happily said yes.

When the couple arrived in California, it just seemed to make sense for them to move into an apartment together. It would save them a lot of money. They loved being together. They were busy running Justin's campaign for city council. And because they assumed they were going to get married sometime in the future, living together would help them make sure they were right for each other.

## CHAPTER 1

# first comes Love, then comes marriage

Rachel was one of the trainers at the gym where I worked out, and I often asked her for exercise advice. She would say such things as, "Tuck that tummy." "Get your elbows in." "Your breathing is backwards!" And my favorite: "How long have you been working out?" My progress has not always been evident to the masses.

While exercising, Rachel and I would often carry on conversations about anything and everything. Over the course of our three-year "gym friendship" we had many interesting discussions about school, careers, money, marriage and God—you name it, we probably talked about it. Rachel was an easy person to chat with, and she must have felt safe around me. She often opened up, sharing a lot about her personal life.

At 23, Rachel was near the end of her college years. She was still living at home with her parents, and she was looking forward to the day when she would be out on her own.

On one particular day when I asked, "How ya doin'?" Rachel initially gave me the stock reply, "Great!" That is what people usually say when someone greets them with that question. But then Rachel added an unexpectedly emotion-filled statement.

"Dave," she said, "I've been dating my boyfriend now for almost two years."

"Wow, it's been that long?"

"Yes," she replied. "He's a wonderful person, and I'm hoping we'll get married someday."

I casually added, "Great! I'd like to meet him."

I went back to another agonizing set of bicep curls. Just as I pulled up my last one (every curl is painful for me and it always feels like my arms are about to fall off!), Rachel spoke again. "It's still kind of hard to believe, but my boyfriend and I have decided that we are going to live together."

The enthusiasm in her voice projected how thrilled she was. She wanted me to be one of the first to know.

Rachel explained that neither of them had ever planned on living together. But after talking about it for quite a while, it just seemed like the right thing to do. In her mind, it was a surprising new direction for their lives.

To be honest, I was surprised, too. *Really surprised.* Given what she had said all along about marriage, I had no idea she would even consider living with someone before walking down the aisle. You might think, *Whew, are you out of touch, Dave!* OK, I am no longer a wide-eyed youth; but I am a Baby Boomer, I lived through the 1960s, and over the years I have talked with literally hundreds of couples. I certainly had clues about the trend but was surprised to discover just how common the to-live-together-or-not quandary had become.

## WHAT THE FACTS REVEAL

Before 1970 it was illegal in every state for a man and a woman to live together if they were not married. It is no wonder Linda LeClair and Peter Behr made newspaper headlines in 1968.

Linda was a sophomore at Barnard College. Peter was a Columbia University undergraduate. These two unwed 20-year-old college students did something that millions of Americans found newsworthy. *They admitted they were living together.* Newspapers and magazines relayed the shocking news. They were shacking up in an off-campus apartment in violation of Barnard College's regulations.

If Linda and Peter's living together were to occur today, most people would probably say, "So what? Lots of people live together." What was once uncommon has become commonplace. Barnard College no longer has a regulation that prohibits unmarried couples living together off campus. As you can probably guess, the state of New York no longer has a law that prohibits unmarried couples from living together anywhere. However, the surprise today is that eight states still do.[1]

New Mexico is one such state. For nearly 150 years, a state law has prohibited unwed couples from cohabitation. But in April 2000, when a woman tried to impose that law on her ex-husband—who was living with another woman—the authorities would not charge him. District Attorney Mike Runnels said, "It's not in anybody's best interest to have the courts clogged with this kind of a case."[2] He was saying that times have changed. The law is old. If they were to start charging people for this crime, the courts would be packed with couples who live together.

*We are moving from a "marriage culture" to a "living together culture."*

GLENN STANTON

### An Ever-Increasing Number

What used to be, no longer is. Things have radically changed over the last 30 years. Before 1970, most couples married before they lived together. Today most couples live together before they marry. And now many couples who live together never even intend to marry. As shown below, the number of unmarried couples who live together is increasing at an alarming rate.

| Year | Number of Unmarried Couples Living Together |
|------|---------------------------------------------|
| 1970 | 523,000 |
| 1980 | 1,589,000 |
| 1990 | 2,856,000 |
| 2000 | 5,500,000[3] |

## Graph 1.1

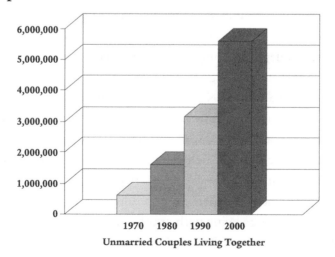

Unmarried Couples Living Together

Since 1970 the number of unmarried-couple households has increased 952 percent.[4] The numbers grew by 204 percent between 1970 and 1980, 80 percent from 1980 to 1990, and 93 percent from 1990 to 2000. Today almost everyone can say they know people who are unmarried and living together.

*I don't like the institution of marriage. I don't think it is good for women. And I don't think any woman should ever get married. Just live with a guy.*

ROSEANNE ARNOLD, INTERVIEWED BY DAVID LETTERMAN

## A Typical Neighborhood

Nearly two decades ago, my wife and I moved into a home in a typical middle-class Southern California suburb. Because we lived there for so long, we saw neighbors move in, stay for a while and then move away. Throughout the time we lived in that neighborhood, one thing never changed. There was always at least one unmarried couple living in one of the houses immediately around ours.

# WHAT MOST COUPLES DO

Recently I was speaking with a friend who is a psychiatrist. He is 68 years old.

"Doc," I said, "how ya doin'?"

His reply was typical. "Great," he said. "I just finished playing two hours of tennis."

I was impressed. I would have been lying on the floor after playing that long, but he was invigorated and ready to meet the day. Then he added, "Singles." He had played two hours of singles tennis at 68 years old! I would love to be able to do that when I am 68. In fact, I would like to be able to do that now!

"Where do you get all your energy?" I asked. I was thinking he had a secret diet or supplement that my wife would just love to start me on!

He said, "It seems to be genetic. Or maybe it just goes back to my days when I grew up on a farm. Being tired was never an excuse. You just had to keep going from sunrise to sunset."

Doc is a fun guy to be around. He jumps at the chance to make a difference with his life. Even now, after all these years, he still enthusiastically sees up to eight clients a day. He loves what he does. Moreover, he always seems to be clued in on what is happening in couples' lives. Having now practiced psychiatry for more than 40 years, he's been able to see firsthand how family life has changed in America.

Doc asked me what my Palm Pilot was telling me I would be doing that day. I told him I was going to spend some time writing this book. His reply gave me a firsthand window of insight into his experience with couples.

"Dave," he said, "almost all of the couples I see in my practice today are unmarried couples living together. Things have really changed. It's just the way things are now. They live together before they marry; that is, if they ever do marry."

Doc's observation can be supported by the facts. Today, most couples who marry live together first.

- 11 percent of couples lived together before marriage in 1970.[5]
- 50 percent or more of couples lived together before marriage in 1995.[6]

These numbers are not surprising when you poll today's teenagers. Although 90 percent of them say they believe in marriage, 74 percent say they would live with someone before marriage or instead of marriage. They say, "If things don't work out, we can chalk it up to experience and move on. At least we will have learned something about ourselves and marriage."[7]

**Graph 1.2**

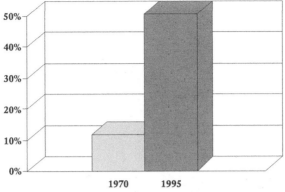

Couples That Live Together Before Marriage

# HOW CHILDREN ENTER THE MIX

I remember singing a nursery rhyme when I was a child. We usually pulled it out at a time when we wanted to inflict emotional harm on one of our friends who showed any interest in the opposite gender. Perhaps you sang it, too. It went like this:

Bob and Bettie sitting in a tree
K-I-S-S-I-N-G.
First comes love,
Then comes marriage,
Then comes baby in a baby carriage.

*I don't think a father is necessary to raise a healthy, happy baby.*

JODIE FOSTER

This rhyme was more than just child's play. It was descriptive of the way things used to be. First love, then marriage, then a baby. Most couples used to marry before they had children. What used to be, no longer is.

Are you ready for another big surprise? For the first time in sixty years of data collection, the United States Census Bureau

## Graph 1.3

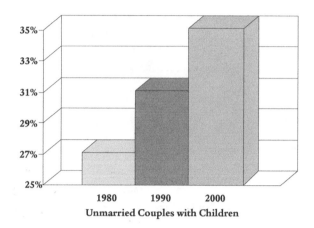

**Unmarried Couples with Children**

found that the majority of firstborn children are now born out of wedlock.[8] Back in the 1930s the figure was only 18 percent.[9]

Today there are more than 1.4 million unmarried couples living together with children under the age of 15.[10] This number has been steadily rising since 1980.

- In 1980, 27 percent of unmarried couples living together had children.
- In 1990, 31 percent of unmarried couples living together had children.
- In 2000, 35 percent of unmarried couples living together had children.[11]

Of these couples living together with children:

- One-third have never been married.
- One-half were previously married.
- One-sixth have had one or more children since living together.[12]

Among adults ages 25 to 34 who are living together but are not married, the percentage of homes in which children are present rose from 34 percent in 1980 to 47 percent in 1990.[13]

The way things were is no longer the way things are. Today it's love first, then child-bearing and then marriage—maybe.

## HOW RELIGION AFFECTS THE DECISION

Perhaps the most surprising change among unmarried couples is found among those who claim to be religious or born-again. Now two, and sometimes three, out of every five couples who claim to be religious are living together unmarried.

One Michigan pastor in an urban ministry said, "Every single couple that has come to me for premarital counseling over the past five years has already been living together."[14] My own pastoral experience throughout the past 20 years has paralleled the two out of five ratio. Twenty years ago I rarely saw a couple that was living together come to me and ask me to marry them. Now one out of every two or three couples that come to me for premarital counseling is already living together.

> *The most important thing is to have love. That happens with a marriage, without a marriage, with a single parent, whatever.*
>
> MADONNA

While the percentage of couples living together is higher when the pair does not have strong religious beliefs, the gap is narrowing. According to national researcher George Barna, the percentage of couples living together encompasses:

- 25 percent of those who claim to be born-again Christians
- 37 percent of those who call themselves Christian but did not have beliefs that classified them as born again
- 36 percent of those who attend a Catholic church

- 30 percent of those who attend a Protestant church
- 42 percent of those who associate with a faith other than Christianity
- 45 percent for nonreligious Americans
- 51 percent of those who claim to be atheists[15]

**Graph 1.4**

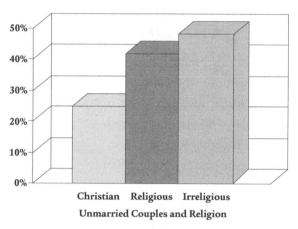

Christian    Religious    Irreligious
**Unmarried Couples and Religion**

# WHAT THE BOTTOM LINE IS

Today more couples are living together than ever before. It does not matter whether or not they hold religious beliefs. Nor does it matter whether they have children or intend to marry some-day. All kinds of people are living together before marriage.

When Rachel told me that morning at the gym that she was going to be moving in with her boyfriend, I asked her why they had made that decision.

While we halfheartedly continued our workouts, she talked about her reasons for moving in with her boyfriend. For the next 10 minutes, Rachel's enthusiasm gushed out. She could hardly wait to make the move.

Her reasons were the same as those given by many cohabiting couples, including Ryan and Amy, whom we meet in chapter 2.

C H A P T E R    2

# the five Reasons

Three months after Ryan met Amy, they moved into Ryan's home. For the next four years they lived together as an unmarried couple.

"When I think back on our decision to live together," Ryan said, "it just made sense. We were in love. I needed a roommate. Amy needed a place to live. And we were probably going to get married someday. Living together would help us figure out if we were really right for each other."

On the afternoon when Ryan and I met to talk about his experience of living with Amy, he had just finished a long day of work. He purchased a large protein-juice drink, and we sat together outside and enjoyed a clear, warm Southern California day. After Ryan told me a little bit about his work as an electrical contractor, we spent the next 90 minutes talking about his relationship with Amy.

Ryan and Amy met through Ryan's brother. Actually, they met while she was *dating* Ryan's brother. Amy was 19; Ryan was 26. "Even though she was younger than me, we were really attracted to each other," he told me. "We had a lot in common."

"So tell me about the time while you were dating, before you decided to live together," I replied.

"Well, we hit it off right from the start. We *loved* being together. We just enjoyed each other's company. We had a lot of fun going places. She liked doing what I liked doing. And from the moment we met, we felt something special—like we could end up getting married someday."

"Moving from dating to living together is a big step. How did you end up deciding to live together?" I asked.

"It *was* big." Ryan replied. "But we had to do it. You see, we had already started talking about getting married someday. In fact we talked about marriage a lot. But before that could happen, *we wanted to be sure*. I also wanted my new electrical company to stabilize financially. And there were some things I saw in Amy that I wanted to help her deal with before we got married. So living together first just made sense."

Ryan's reasons for asking Amy to move in with him, rather than getting married first, are some of the common reasons couples give for living together today. They are the same rationale Rachel gave for her and her boyfriend's decision.

When asked, couples most often point to the same five primary reasons for living together before marriage.

# REASON NUMBER ONE: EXPERIENCE

*We are living together to find out if we are compatible with each other.*
Would you buy a car without first taking it out for a test-drive? Most people would not. I know I never have and probably never will. It only makes sense to check it out for yourself. Does it meet your expectations? Is it comfortable? Will it make you happy? Test-drive before you buy.

A growing number of couples feel the same way about marriage. Before jumping into a lifelong commitment, they want to make sure they are compatible with each other. To them it seems to make sense that the best way to find out is to live together for a while and check each other out.

*A study in the* Washington Post *says that women have better verbal skills than men. I just want to say to the authors of that study—Duh!*

CONAN O'BRIEN

This is the number one reason couples live together before marriage. They want to find out firsthand if they are really compatible. Up to this point they think they are, but they want to be sure.

For some, living together has become a test run. Before people take the marriage plunge, they want to make sure the water is warm. They have seen too many divorces. If they get married, they want to covenant for life. They want to decrease the chances of divorce and increase the chances of a strong until-death-do-us-part marriage.

A girl who had been dating a guy for several years asked a counselor if she should live with the guy before they got married. The counselor replied,

I lived with my husband for several years before we married, and I would not have done otherwise. I think marriage is such a serious business that it makes sense to gather as much information as possible before tying the knot. Living together can tell two people a lot about how compatible they are and their ability to negotiate their differences.[1]

According to a Gallup poll contracted by Rutgers University, 62 percent of men and women in their 20s agree with this counselor and believe living together before marriage is a good way to avoid divorce. Another 42 percent say they would only marry someone if that person agreed to live together first.[2] "It's a test run," said Kit Russell of Goleta, California, who expects to wed her live-in partner and is convinced that the experience saved her from a disastrous marriage to a previous boyfriend.[3]

> *All men make mistakes, but married men find out about them sooner.*
>
> RED SKELTON

## REASON NUMBER TWO: FINANCES

*We are living together because it makes good sense financially.*

This is the second most common reason couples give for living together—two can live together cheaper than one, they reason; why pay for two homes when we can live in one?

Housing is certainly less expensive. Cooking for two costs less than two people dining on their own. Utilities—electricity, garbage, water, telephone and the like—are cheaper when shared.

Two people living together for economic reasons often intend to split their expenses 50-50. Interestingly, sociologist Roland Johnson and others have found that women more often than men end up contributing the most—often as much as 70 percent.[4]

Moreover, some couples live together for tax or inheritance reasons. Many unmarried senior citizens live this way because of tax disincentives to marry. Others' incomes place them into a tax bracket that allows for greater deductions if they remain single.

Among couples who have lived together in my own neighborhood, financial reasons have been the primary reason for doing so. More often than not, their decision was based on being able to buy or rent a house. With the average price of a home continuing to escalate, pooling financial resources has made it possible for some to get into a home.

## REASON NUMBER THREE: COMPANIONSHIP

*We would rather live with someone we love than live alone.*

In the beginning, after God created the first man, He said, "It is not good for the man to be alone" (Gen. 2:18). Most singles I know would agree with God. They may not be ready to make a lifelong commitment, but they would rather be living with someone they love than living alone. One of my two brothers has lived by himself for 20 years. Even after two decades of being single, he would still rather live with and share his life with a woman.

> *Being in therapy is great. I spend an hour just talking about myself. It's kinda like being the guy on a date.*
>
> CAROLINE RHEA

One of my single friends, even though he leads an active life, still battles loneliness. Coming home to an empty house is an emotional test. He longs to be with someone he can love for life. Some couples choose to live together to combat these kinds of real emotional struggles.

There are a number of emotional reasons why a couple may choose to live together without getting married, but the need to eliminate loneliness is prominent.

Some people say they move in together because of their need to feel loved and appreciated. Although not ready for lifelong vows, they want the security that they think living together will provide. This need may not only be emotional but also sexual.

A few people feel obligated to live with their partner for fear of losing him or her. They may succumb to the pressure and simply go along with it because their partner—for whatever reason—wants them to live together.

## Reason Number Four: Culture

*We want to live together because nowadays everyone lives together before they get married.*

Historically society frowned on couples who lived together outside of marriage. Today the pendulum has swung to the other extreme. If two people choose *not* to live together before marriage, many think they are strange—out of step, old-fashioned, a quart low.

The societal, parental and religious influences and pressures that once held a strong hand in keeping couples apart until marriage have weakened. When the television show *Three's Company* appeared in 1977, most Americans were shocked. In the show, two single women and a single man share an apartment. Even though the three characters were not physically involved, it was rare that individuals of the opposite sex would live together under the same roof. Today that concern is laughable. Now it is commonplace for males and females to reside together, whether they are romantically involved, just friends or a combination of both!

Today there is even social pressure *to* live together. Couples are told, "Everyone else is doing it. How else will you know if you should get married? You don't want to end up with the wrong guy (or girl)!"

Even a growing number of parents see nothing wrong with unmarried couples living together. In fact, they often agree, saying it's a great idea. Many parents are intimately aware of the pain of divorce. Therefore, to them, living together first just seems like the smart move.

Even religious beliefs have changed for some. It used to be understood in churches and among people who attended them that couples should not live together until marriage. End of discussion! Not so anymore. Many who come to a church to be married are already living together. This culturally accepted practice no longer stands in the way of their being married in the church.

There are also some people who hold what has been called antimarriage sentiments. These are people who are deliberately seeking an alternative to traditional marriage. They are not simply living together before marriage. They are living together *instead* of getting married. They believe marriage is pointless and irrelevant. They see marriage as being repressive, dated and unnecessary.

> *Cultural acceptance and science have broken the old tight equation of marriage and child rearing. All forms of families are claiming legitimacy and, to some extent, are getting it.*
>
> STEPHANIE COONTZ,
> COUNCIL ON
> CONTEMPORARY
> FAMILIES

## REASON NUMBER FIVE: LOVE

*We're going to get married eventually. We're in love.*

The fact is most men and women who live together as a couple *do* plan to get married. If they did not, they probably would not have decided to share a home. Some are not engaged yet, but they anticipate making that commitment—someday. Some are already engaged. Some have set the wedding date and are counting the days.

Other couples speak about how they *are* in love. Couples in love often feel as though they are doing nothing wrong by living together. They reason that as long as it is a good thing for both of them, why not? Why wait for marriage?

Over the years I have found that couples usually look at how they answer two questions—Do we love each other? and, Are we going to get married someday anyway?—as the final analysis before they decide to move in together. As long as they answer yes to both questions, they feel that living together will be a strong plus in building their relationship. They conclude their desire to be married someday, along with their love for each other, are reasons enough to live together. Surely this, in part, explains why today more than 50 percent of couples live together before marriage.

That was certainly the case with Ryan and Amy. They wanted to be sure. Today they are sure—sure they will never marry. While Amy was living with Ryan, she met Ryan's friend and slept with him.

"Depressed," "hurt," "grieving"—just a few words that describe how Ryan feels today. With how things turned out, Ryan is glad he never married Amy. But now he wishes he had never lived with her either.

"Bad start. Bad ending. You can't expect it to be much different than that," he said. "At this point, in my next relationship I'd definitely do things different than I did this time. I'd rather not go through anything like this again. It hurts too much."

Ryan and Amy had been told, "Live together to find out if you are compatible." Theoretically, it sounded like a good idea. And they *did* find out what they wanted to know, but they had not been warned about the painful consequences in the real world.

C H A P T E R    3

# Welcome to the
# Real World

For more than a decade, Agoura Bible Fellowship in Agoura, California—where I served on staff for almost 25 years—annually hosted a Christmas Dinner Theater. It has become a community highlight. People from all faiths and beliefs come. Most are first invited as guests and then return year after year. It is a great way to spend an enjoyable evening with friends and get the Christmas season off to a wonderful start.

Over the years, I brought many people to these dinners. A few years ago I invited another gym friend. He is an older guy who had recently moved in with his girlfriend. This couple, like many today, had decided to live together, even though they would not have done so in the past. Prior to their relationship with each other, their personal and religious beliefs had kept them from living with someone of the opposite sex. Shortly after they moved in together, I asked him what had changed. Why had he decided to live with Karen?

Jim's answer was typical. "Society has really changed. We're no longer living in the Dark Ages. I've been hurt in the past, and this time I want to be sure. And the best way to be sure if Karen and I should get married is to live together first."

The evening of the Christmas Dinner Theater arrived and Jim and Karen had a great time. The following week they sent us a note of thanks and expressed their desire to come again the next year.

My friendship with Jim and Karen continued throughout the following 12 months. Jim and I shared a lot of good conversations and laughs as we worked out together. As far as I could tell, his relationship with Karen seemed to be going well. Throughout that year I was just waiting to hear the news that they would soon be marrying.

When November rolled around and I posed my usual "How ya doin'?" question to Jim, he said, "Dave, things aren't going well."

"Would you like to talk about it?" I offered.

"No," he quickly answered, "not now; maybe later. But thanks for asking."

Over the years, Jim and I have talked about many subjects. Our past conversations gave me ample insight about the time and place to speak with him about personal and professional matters. Jim would talk when Jim wanted to talk, so I let it go. But knowing the Christmas dinner was just around the corner, I decided to see if he and Karen were still interested in coming again. I thought it would be something fun and positive to talk about—something safe. Whew, was I wrong.

I said, "Hey, Jim, I've got some extra tickets for this year's Christmas dinner. You mentioned last year that you'd like to go again. Would you like me to hold tickets for you and Karen?"

"I'm not celebrating Christmas this year," Jim said.

"Wow, how does Karen feel about that?"

Then came the bombshell. Jim said, "I don't know. She left me a week ago."

With those few words, Jim opened up and we had a long conversation about his loss. He was really hurting. He said he did not see it coming. He was blindsided by the whole thing. He came home one day and found that Karen had moved out. All her things were gone. She had left him and moved in with another man.

Jim is still processing this whole mess. He still hurts. It is doubtful he will ever live with someone outside of marriage again.

Though the majority of people think that living together *sounds* like a good idea, the statistics show that it is not. This has been substantiated by many studies that have focused on the effects on those who have lived together. There are five primary reasons why most authorities today say living together is very unwise.

> *Cohabitation—It's training for divorce.*
>
> CHUCK COLSON

# REASON NUMBER ONE: GREATER CHANCE FOR DIVORCE

If you want to *increase* your no-divorce odds, you are better off not living together before marriage. Approximately 50 percent of all couples that marry end up getting a divorce. But 75 percent (three out of four) of the couples that live together before marriage end up divorced. Your chances of divorcing are *increased* rather than decreased by living together before marriage.

It seems that couples that live together before marriage would be less likely to get a divorce, but studies prove otherwise.

- A national study of 1,800 married couples found divorce was twice as high in cases where the couple had lived together before marriage.[1]
- A study of 3,884 women who lived with their mates before marriage found that 50 percent were more likely to get a divorce than those who first married before living together.[2]
- One study at Yale University found the risk of divorce after living together before marriage to be as high as 80 percent.[3]
- A study of 3,300 adults found that a couple that lives together before marriage is 46 percent more likely to divorce.[4]
- Unmarried cohabitations overall are less stable than marriages. The probability of a first marriage ending in separation or divorce within five years is 20 percent, but the probability of a premarital cohabitation breaking up within five years is 49 percent. After 10 years, the probability of a first marriage ending is 33 percent, compared with 62 percent for cohabitations.[5]
- A University of Denver study found that a cohabiting couple has a significantly higher rate of divorce than a couple that does not live together first.[6]
- *U.S. News and World Report* concluded that a cohabiting couple that marries is about 33 percent more likely to divorce than a couple that does not live together before exchanging nuptials.[7]

One researcher summarized his findings with these words:

> The popular belief that cohabitation is an effective strategy in a high-divorce society rests on the commonsense notion that getting to know one another before marrying should improve the quality and stability of marriage. However, in this instance, it is looking more and more as if common sense is a poor guide.[8]

> *I really wish I'd never lived with my ex-husband first. He might not be my ex today. I hope my son decides against it, also, when that time comes.*
>
> ANONYMOUS

There are exceptions to the trend revealed in the studies. One college student said her parents lived together for three years prior to marriage. Now they have been married for 25 years. True, one out of four couples does make it—but the odds are against it.

## REASON NUMBER TWO: BETTER ODDS FOR CONFLICT

Living together outside marriage increases the risk of emotional and physical abuse. Dr. Jan Stets of Washington State University concluded that "aggression is at least twice as common among cohabitors as it is among married partners."[9] A Pennsylvania State University study found that unmarried couples living together argue, shout and hit each other more than married couples do.[10]

At an international conference on personal relationships in Brisbane, Australia, Catherine Cohan, Ph.D., reported the results of another study conducted by Pennsylvania State University. This professor of human development and family studies found that couples that live together outside of marriage "tend to have poorer communication skills once married, which may in turn increase their likelihood of divorce."[11]

*Love begins with a smile, grows with a kiss, and ends with a teardrop.*

ANONYMOUS

Couples participating in the study were each given a list of common personal and marital problems. The list included sexual difficulties, money, career decisions, religion and family planning. Once couples had selected a relevant problem, they were asked to discuss and attempt to solve it while being videotaped.

After examining the videotapes, Cohan discovered the following:

Cohabiting couples displayed more negative and fewer positive problem-solving and support behaviors than couples who had not cohabited prior to marriage. In particular, when discussing a topic the husband had identified as a problem, partners who had cohabited tended to express more negative behaviors such as coerciveness and attempts to control. And in general, wives who had lived with their partners prior to marriage were generally more verbally aggressive than those couples with no premarital cohabitation.[12]

This kind of domestic violence has risen dramatically over the past 40 years. Prior to 1960, when virtually no one lived together before they got married, domestic violence was relatively low. But now, with a growing number of unmarried people living together as a couple, domestic violence is on the rise. While this may not account for all of the factors involved in domestic violence, the results for people who live together have been tragic.

- According to the U.S. Justice Department, women are 62 times more likely to be assaulted if living with a man unmarried than if they were married.[13]

- The Family Violence Research Program at the University of New Hampshire found that the overall rate for "severe" violence is nearly 6 times as high for cohabiting couples than it is for married couples.[14]
- The National Crime Victimization Survey revealed that between 1979 and 1987, 65 percent of violent crimes against women were committed by boyfriends or ex-husbands, while only 9 percent were committed by a husband.[15]

## REASON NUMBER THREE: LESS CHANCE FOR HAPPINESS

Unmarried couples that live together have lower levels of happiness than married couples, both before and during marriage.

It is hard for a person to be happy when his or her relationship is built on the need to prove himself or herself. Yet when a boyfriend and girlfriend decide to live together before marriage, often they do so to prove their love and compatibility to one another. In this arrangement, commitment is day-to-day and month-to-month. "If" is the watchword: *If* you make me happy—*If* we are sexually compatible—*If* you meet my needs. Jessie Shirley Bernard addresses this concern in her book *The Future of Marriage*:

> People who marry "til death do us part" have quite a different level of commitment, therefore quite a different level of security, thus a quite different level of freedom, and as a result a quite different level of happiness than those who marry "so long as love doth last." The love-doth-last folks are always anticipating the moment when they or their mate wakes up one morning and

finds the good feeling that holds them afloat has dissolved beneath them.[16]

It is no wonder that in a study of 6,203 couples, married partners reported significantly higher levels of happiness than did cohabiting partners.[17] Many other studies have found that marriage offers a couple a huge advantage in mental and emotional health. Married men and women report less depression, less anxiety and lower levels of other types of psychological distress than do those who are single, divorced or widowed.[18] One study concluded that cohabiting couples have significantly weaker relationships than married couples.[19]

*Sex takes the least amount of time, but causes the most amount of trouble.*

MARK TWAIN

The effects of cohabitation on women have been well documented:

- According to the National Institute for Mental Health, women who cohabit with men have rates of depression three times higher than married women.
- Nearly 25 percent of women who cohabit with men suffer from neurotic disorders, compared to 15 percent of married women.
- Women who cohabit with men are more irritable, anxious, worried and unhappy than married women.[20]

When it comes to sexual happiness, unmarried partners are at higher risk of being hurt by the other's unfaithfulness. One study reported in *Sexual Attitudes and Lifestyles* indicated that 90 percent of married men *and* married women were monogamous. But among the unmarried, only 60 percent of women and 43 percent of men stayed true to their partner.[21] The National Sex

Survey found that men who lived with women were about four times more likely than husbands to report infidelity in the past year. Women who lived with men were eight times more likely than wives to cheat on their partners.[22] It is no wonder that some have said living together before marriage is a setup for a lot of unhappiness and hurt.

## REASON NUMBER FOUR: GREATER RISK OF ADULTERY

A National Council on Family Relations study found that newlyweds who first cohabited were less happy or satisfied in marriage than those who had not lived together.[23] Dr. Joyce Brothers adds, "Cohabitation has a negative effect on the quality of a subsequent marriage."[24] A Michigan study shows that couples who waited to cohabit until after marriage were more likely to rate their relationships stronger than those who lived together before marriage.[25]

Sexual faithfulness is one of the many areas negatively impacted. If a woman lives with a man before marriage, she is more likely to cheat on him once they are married. The *Journal of Marriage and the Family* found that women between the ages of 20 and 37 who had lived with their partner before marriage were 3.3 times more likely to have an extramarital affair.[26] Men are also more likely to cheat once they are married. This definitely has an impact on the happiness levels in a marriage.

> *Men are not supposed to see only one woman and only desire one woman. . . . That's just science. If the species don't [sic] mutate, it'll die. This is a man. This is what he's on Earth for.*
>
> GOLDIE HAWN

Contrary to popular belief, the best sex is not experienced by unmarried people. The National Sex Survey of 3,500 people[27] and another survey of 1,000 people[28] concluded that married people have more and better sex than singles do. A husband and wife have sex more often and enjoy it more than those who are unmarried. A long-term marital commitment deepens emotional and physical satisfaction, even over decades of marriage. Studies by Dr. Evelyn Duvall and Dr. Judson Landis resulted in the same conclusion: Premarital sex is not as satisfying as marital sex.

Sexual happiness is also connected to whether or not a couple saves sex for marriage. Those who do wait are 29 to 47 percent more likely to enjoy it within marriage. The Family Research Council found that 72 percent of these couples report higher sexual satisfaction.[29]

# REASON NUMBER FIVE: LESS LIKELIHOOD OF SAYING "I DO"

A common reason couples give for living together is that they are going to get married anyway. This was certainly the case with the couple I described at the beginning of this chapter. Their feeling was, *Why wait?*

Some people planning to marry move in together for financial reasons. Up to this point they have been living in two separate homes. Why continue paying for two places? Why not put all of their hard-earned dollars into one place right now?

My professional experience has given me many opportunities to work with couples that are planning on marriage.

When a couple comes to me for premarital counseling, they usually already have their plans set. They are committed to marry. They have chosen the date. They want me to help them prepare for their marriage. They want to do all they can to be ready for a long, happy union.

A couple's engagement can be a wonderful time. It can also be a very revealing time. For Brandon and Heidi it was filled with emotional highs and lows. They were certain they were right for each other and that their love would take them through whatever hardships might be ahead. But the fact is their engagement period ultimately convinced them that they should not get married.

I had the privilege of meeting with Brandon and Heidi for three months. Our focus was on matters that build healthy marriages. We spent time talking about communication, conflict resolution, expectations, needs, personality issues and spiritual compatibility. These topics ultimately raised so many issues between them that they called the whole thing off—but not without a lot of emotional pain. It was tough to let go of their hope to spend the rest of their lives together.

If you had the opportunity to speak with Brandon and Heidi today, they would tell you they are glad they did not marry. What they went through as an engaged couple—not living together—was painful. But it would have been even more agonizing had they been living together at the time—and even worse if they had gotten married anyway, only to end up getting a divorce later.

Only about one out of two couples that live together ultimately marry each other. According to Brown and Booth, only 50 to 60 percent of first-time cohabitors marry the person with whom they live[30]— in spite of the fact that 70 to 90 percent of couples that live together say they *intend* to marry each other (or at least one of them feels this way).[31] Other studies have shown similar or even worse findings. Researchers Casper and Bianchi concluded that "after five to seven years, 39 percent of all cohabiting couples have broken their relationship, 40 percent have married (although the marriage might not have lasted) and only 21 percent are still cohabiting."[32] A National Survey of Families and

> *I have a very strong feeling that the opposite of love is not hate—it's apathy.*
>
> DR. LEO BUSCAGLIA

Households, based on interviews with 13,000 people, concluded that "about 40 percent of cohabiting unions in the U.S. break up without the couple getting married."[33]

Living together before marriage actually decreases the chances that a couple will marry. The odds are greater that they will not. *Are you sure you want to put yourself through that possibility and the pain that follows?*

## STRONGER CHOICE IN HIGH-RISK, LOW-REWARD OPTION

If you had a choice between high risk and low reward, or low risk and high reward, which would you choose? I would go with the latter—every time!

Is living together before you are married such a good idea? Think about it in terms of the risk-benefit factor. If you and your girlfriend or boyfriend cohabit your chances

for divorce are 50 percent greater;
for aggression, 50 percent greater;
of *not* marrying, 50 percent greater.

If you knew your chances of failure were compounded by 50 percent, would you add greater risk to something that is already risky? Would you parachute from an airplane if you knew one out of every two chutes would fail? Probably not. You might be willing to jump under normal risk factors, but adding an unnecessary 50 percent failure rate would probably make even the bravest among us pass on that thrill.

I believe the statistics show the wise choice is to marry first and then live together. Your chances for happiness now and later are greater if you do. I hope that by marrying first, you would be spared the pain the following person experienced:

I am in a cohabitation relationship going on a year now and I love the person dearly but living together is just not enough for me anymore and I want marriage but in a way I think that he is just comfortable the way things are now and I feel as if he could make me wait forever. I will never do this again should my boyfriend and I break up. I just feel like I am doing all that a wife does and more and I don't get anything out of it. The stats scare me considering that we are currently engaged I just am frightened. I don't even want to marry him now. I just want to move out and start over.[34]

# Rehearsal for marriage

Today most people who consider marriage want to do all they can to ensure a no-divorce future. They do not want to fall into the meet-marry-divorce pattern. Some have experienced up close the awful consequences of broken homes. Others have seen the consequences from a distance. Whatever their firsthand encounters have been, unmarried people know divorce hurts, and they would like to do all they can to prevent it from ever happening to them.

Divorce prevention is high on the list of reasons why people choose to live together before walking down the aisle. By cohabiting they hope to find out if their future marriage will make it.

Furthermore, they do not want to live like so many people whose marriages are miserable—painfully enduring each day as an unhappily married couple.

## LIVING TOGETHER: A TEST RUN?

The price tag is high when matrimony does not work out. Hoping to make the right decision, many couples have turned to the try-before-you-buy approach: Living together seems like a good way to check each other out.

If we try something before we buy it, our chances of satisfaction are greater than if we simply buy it off the shelf. Purchasing something because it looks really good, even something as common as a sofa, can disappoint us later if we have never sat on it. Whether it is a new car, perfume, pair of shoes or flavor of ice cream, we all want to try it out first. If we like it, we will go ahead and buy it. After all, who wants to be stuck with something they do not like? In marriage the stakes are obviously much higher than with ice cream or shoes.

### The Tryout

I enjoy playing golf, but like many people I have had my share of horrible-no-good-very-bad-always-in-the-rough days. Fortunately, I have also enjoyed a few of the better days, when everything goes right. I admit they are rare—really rare. But when they happen, I'm lovin' life.

A few years ago I was in the market for a golf club. I thought a new driver would give me a few extra yards off the tee. After reading and hearing about the latest golf technology, I thought I would play better if I garaged my woods and purchased a new metal driver.

I do not really enjoy shopping. My philosophy is simple: Get in, get it done, and get out of the store as quickly and debt-free as possible. In my quest for the perfect driver I found a golf shop that allows people to try before they buy. For five dollars, a customer can take any demo driver out to the golf course and give it a swing. If someone so desired, he or she could try out every demo driver in the store before settling on one. Once a decision to purchase is made, every five dollars already paid out on the test-run drivers is deducted from the final cost. That is my kind of deal!

*A Harris poll has found that 79 percent of both the single men and women surveyed rated "intelligence" as the most important characteristic in their potential mates. 70 percent of both sexes rated "funny" in second place. Both rated "attractive" in third place at 34 percent, "athletic" at 12 percent and "wealthy" at 6 percent.*

"AMERICAN DEMOGRAPHICS," *WASHINGTON TIMES*

For a month I tried out club after club. Finally I found a driver that fit me perfectly. Made with the latest technology, it gave me hope of actually posting some lower scores.

I purchased and still have the driver. I occasionally use it. But I am thinking about shopping again. You see, my "perfect" driver is not so perfect after all. I still hit the ball out-of-bounds. Sometimes it has helped my golf game. More often than not, I do not even take it out of my golf bag. But it is still mine, and I cannot take it back. Now I am stuck with it.

The idea of trying someone out like we would test a golf club or car is crude. No way! Most people would never stoop that low. And they certainly would not live with someone who was simply trying them out. The thought is offensive. "Don't even go there," you would probably say.

But, if I may, let me ask you to *go there* with me. Let's try to understand what a person hopes to experience, or find out, by living with a boyfriend or girlfriend. What really motivates him or her to cohabit instead of getting married?

## The Compatibility Test

Let's look at the average unmarried couple: Both partners surely think they are in love with the other. They believe it is the kind of love that *could* lead to marriage, but they want to be sure. They are not yet ready to make the big commitment. They want to find out if they are right for each other—to see if it really will work—so they decide to live together and see how it goes. One of them agrees to move in with the other and the tryout begins.

Call it what you like, but living together is really a tryout, or audition—a test that goes both ways. She is trying him out; he is trying her out. She wants to know if he is good enough; he wants to know if she is good enough—but good enough for what? To one day get married and spend the rest of their lives together. If the other person does not pass that test, then he or she will just move on.

How does one person know if the other is right for him or her? The surface answer is "We'll know we're right for each other if we are compatible, if we are both happy and fulfilled." What it really means is "It all depends on whether or not my partner meets my expectations." Living together works as long as each person satisfies the other's needs—as long as the other person is able to live up to the expected, and often unspoken, performance standards.

Living together automatically puts two people into a performance-based relationship. Each person attempts to earn the other's love through achievement. Each evaluates whether the other meets up to his or her expectations.

Two words characterize performance-based relationships: "if" and "then." Whether you want to admit it, when two people live together before marriage they are thinking:

- *If* you make me feel loved, *then* I'll marry you.
- *If* you satisfy me sexually, *then* I'll marry you.
- *If* you treat me with respect, *then* I'll marry you.

- *If* you make me happy, *then* I'll marry you.
- *If* you fulfill my needs, *then* I'll marry you.
- *If* you like what I like, *then* I'll marry you.
- *If* you make something of yourself, *then* I'll marry you.
- *If* you don't do things that get on my nerves, *then* I'll marry you.

In and of themselves, all of these *if*s matter in marriage. They *are* important issues. Nothing is wrong with wanting to be loved, to be happy or to have your needs met. But there are two approaches to dealing with these wants: One focuses on *your partner* satisfying *you*, and the second focuses on *you* satisfying *your partner*.

**The Need Meter**
If your focus is on having your needs met, and your partner fails to pass the test, you will move on and find someone else who will. Wade Horn, a columnist for the *Washington Times*, made this clear when he contrasted marriage with living together:

> In marriage, the goal is taking care of the other person, in sickness and in health, for richer and poorer. Contrast this with cohabitation, where the goal is not so much to determine whether I am up to the task of taking care of your needs, but whether you are up to the task of taking care of mine. The "trial" in marriage is not a test of oneself, but a test of the other. When cohabitors assert that they are testing their compatibility for each other, what they really mean is that they are testing how well the other person fulfills their needs.[1]

Trying out a golf club makes sense. It is an inanimate object that does not care what you do or think. If it brings you pleasure, buy it. Keep it for as long as it is useful. But if it stops meeting your needs or falls short of your expectations, bag it, discard it, trade it in or sell it.

Trying out a potential spouse offends the senses. While a golf club is *a product to use*, a potential spouse is *a person to love*. When you live together before marriage, you are actually trying each other out like you would a product. A person, however, is not something to be bagged, discarded, traded in or sold. When your nuptials come first, you are making a mutual commitment for the long haul.

> *A quarter of British couples claim that snoring is ruining their love lives and 10 percent say the problem is so bad they may divorce. About 80 percent of couples say they have resorted to sleeping separately to escape the noise.*
>
> SNOREEZE CENSUS, *BBC*

Statistics show that trying out a potential spouse by living together before marriage actually increases rather than decreases the chances for a divorce. Perhaps the if-then cycle is one of the reasons why. A relationship grounded in the pressure to meet a partner's expectations will only continue along this course into the marriage. No one can live well enough for long enough to satisfy whatever expectations his or her spouse may have.

In a sports tryout, a person must prove that he or she is good enough to make the team. Even if the person makes it, he or she must continue to perform well enough to stay on the team. When your performance slips, you are outta there. A good athlete can handle the pressure for a while, but who can keep performing at an all-star level for a lifetime?

Couples that have healthy marriages build their relationships on a totally different foundation. Whereas the primary basis for living together is to determine if your partner can meet *your* needs, the primary basis of a healthy marriage is sacrificial love.

**The Unconditional Factor**

As we will see in the next chapter, a good marriage is built upon an unconditional commitment to love an imperfect person. The focus is on unconditionally loving the *other* person. Using the golf analogy, in a strong marriage each sees him- or herself as a golf club. In other words, the roles are reversed: The focus is on giving pleasure, not getting it.

> *To love is not a passive thing. To love is active voice. When I love I do something, I function, I give.*
>
> BERNARD IDDINGS BELL

I realize that many of you are thinking, *But what about* my *needs!* They are an important part of the equation, too. But you will have to keep reading to find out how the equation works.

## GROWING TOGETHER: FIVE COMMON RELATIONAL STAGES

People on their way to marriage typically move through five relational stages (see chart below). As their relationship progresses, so do their expectations of deeper commitment and the possibility of deeper pain.

| Commitment Level | Relational Stage | Pain Level |
|---|---|---|
| Low | Acquaintance | Low |
| | Friendship | |
| | Dating | |
| | Engagement | |
| High | Marriage | High |

Unmarried but romantically attached partners say divorce prevention and pain prevention are prominent reasons for living together. They hope that cohabiting before they talk about marriage, or while they are engaged, will keep them from possible pain if things do not work out. They think that the pain of divorce would be greater than simply living together and then breaking up.

*I lost my appetite—I was numb. I literally went to five shrinks, and nothing made sense.*

TARA REID, AFTER HAVING LIVED WITH MTV HOST CARSON DALY

In some ways this may be true. If two people simply lived together and then broke up, they would not have the divorce "label" following them throughout their lives. There also would probably be less of an impact on extended family members.

## The Pain Stakes

The fact is that when a person lives with someone else, whether married or not, there will be great pain if things do not work out. In some ways a cohabiting couple faces even greater chances of pain than they would if they had married and then divorced.

Although the social stigma may be less for those who never married, each person will feel the same pain, and there could be deep emotional scars. There is no getting around those things. There could be

- guilt and shame,
- crushed hopes and dreams,
- financial bondage due to mutual commitments,
- feeling physically used (no one can get that part back),
- a sense of failure (of not being good enough),
- feelings of betrayal (were you deceived?), and
- anger over broken promises.

Have you ever had a boyfriend or a girlfriend break up with you? Did it come without a good explanation? To this day, are you still wondering what happened? Do you remember how you felt? How deeply it hurt?

My heart went out to a girl who wrote for some advice from the columnist Nancy Fagan—who writes under the name Dr. Romance—on how to recover from her own breakup. Her pain is evident in her words:

> Dear Dr. Romance:
> I'm so overwhelmed with my current situation and I truly need your advice. Eight months ago, my boyfriend and I split up after seven years of dating. We were about to get engaged, then suddenly he ended it without much explanation. I feel like he has led me on for all these years.[2]

Dr. Romance responded:

> A man will not date a woman longer than two or three years without getting engaged if he is truly planning on marrying her. A man who does this, has no intention of ever marrying the woman. . . . According to the authors of *What Men Want*, they say that men call this kind of relationship, "good to have around until something better comes along."[3]

I could almost hear the brokenhearted girl say, "But I thought we had something special." Not so if her relationship was a conditional, performance-based commitment. There is nothing special about being judged by how well you measure up. Just think: This letter writer was only in a dating relationship. The stakes get even higher when people move in together—the potential for personal pain dramatically increases.

Pain is a very real part of any relationship. It is inevitable when you share yourself with another person. Then when you bring living together into the dating or engagement stage, you set yourself up for even more pain. What was supposed to be a rehearsal for a lifelong partnership ends up short circuited, and hearts are shattered before any lasting commitment can be made.

---

*Infatuation is when you think that he is as sexy as Robert Redford, as smart as Henry Kissinger, as noble as Ralph Nader, as funny as Woody Allen, and as athletic as Jimmy Connors. Love is when you realize that he's as sexy as Woody Allen, as smart as Jimmy Connors, as funny as Ralph Nader, as athletic as Henry Kissinger, and nothing like Robert Redford—but you'll take him anyway.*

POET JUDITH VIORST

# JUSTIN AND BROOKE: the Rest of the Story

"It started with a kiss on the cheek," Justin reminisced. "And it ended with a kiss on the cheek."

Remember Justin and Brooke? They are the young couple who met in Washington, D.C. After spending several years there—first as friends and then as boyfriend and girlfriend—they decided to move to Justin's hometown in California and begin moving up the ladder in the political world.

When they got to California, they figured it just made sense for them to move in together. Although they had lived separately in Washington, D.C., housing in Southern California is not cheap. Besides, they were in love. Sometimes they felt so connected that they could read each other's minds. They were soul mates. Although they were not yet officially engaged, they—and their families—assumed that marriage was somewhere up ahead.

Justin and I were sitting in the living room of the apartment he had been sharing with Brooke for the past 14 months. It was April and now all was not well. Justin picks up the story:

> Yeah, it was going to happen. I was gonna marry her. Our families were unofficially making plans. The wedding would be in Ohio. My family of California natives had already begun trying to figure out what in the world

they could do in the area around Ohio when they were there. I had told Brooke's mother that if we had to have the wedding in Ohio, I wanted to have the reception on one of those big Mark Twain steamboat things cruising down the Ohio River.

When we got to California, I jumped right in and ran for our local city council. Though it was small-town politics, it was a megajolt of reality regarding what the political world is really like. Wow! Not a lot of glamour—or integrity—there!

And during that time, things started to change between Brooke and me. I didn't feel the support that I would have expected to get from my soul mate. Oh, everyone was still talking as if things were moving ahead in our relationship as usual. But something was different.

After the election (I didn't win—this time!) I took a trip to Washington, D.C., and New York City for five or six days. Just to get away and to visit some friends. When I came back, Brooke met me with a very casual, "Hi, how ya doin'?" I said, "Fine." And that was it. No hug, no kiss, no "Oh, honey, I missed you so much. How are you? How was your trip?"

For me, I think that was the first time I clearly understood that it was over. There was no affection between us at all. We usually gave each other a kiss on the cheek when we left for work or whatever because it was what we were supposed to do. But one day I was so mad at her that I just left. I didn't even give her a kiss good-bye. I guess I was trying to make a statement. The next day I did it again. And that was it. We just stopped kissing. It was over.

As our relationship started deteriorating, Brooke thought things would get better once we got married. And I thought the exact opposite. It would just make things

worse. That's why I'm bailing out. Marriage wouldn't have
made anything better.

Now it was over. Justin and Brooke were counting the days
until they would both move out and away from each other. The
only thing that was keeping them together now was the lease they
had signed on their apartment. Justin continues the sad narrative:

I realized it was over before Brooke did. Or at least before
she admitted it. I just couldn't take it anymore. But
I wasn't sure how to get out of it all. So while everyone
around me was still talking about marriage, I was thinking to myself, *Man, that lease is until June! I really spun
myself a web here. I really screwed up this time.*

So it's April. We're stuck in this lease until June.
Brooke's got a couple of jobs, but it's not even enough to
pay half of our expenses. So we're at the point where I'm
asking her, "Why should I have to pay for you to exist
when all you do is yell at me? I'm not even dating you. We
broke up. You hate me. You yell at me. Then you expect
me to pay $1,200 a month rent?"

We're not in love anymore. We're not dating anymore. So when the lease is up, she wants to erase the past
year of her life, as if the history didn't exist.

At this point, we cannot be in the same room for
more than five seconds without fighting. It's completely
deteriorated to something that feels a lot like hatred—
complete and utter hatred.

It was at about this point that Brooke arrived and joined our
conversation. They were both really hurting. It was obvious. As far
as they were concerned, the sooner they could move on with their
lives, the better. But they wanted me to hear their story. They

sought to share what happened to them, with the hope that others wouldn't go through the same thing. So I asked a lot of questions.

## QUESTIONS AND ANSWERS

**How did you finally break up?**

Brooke began: "Well, our affection for each other . . . slowly but surely died off. But the routine of the relationship continued. In a sense, since we were living together, we were stuck with each other. So the actual breaking up was a slow process. It probably took us four months."

Justin added: "At the beginning of that time Brooke was still thinking that we were getting married, while I was already over it in my heart. I would pray for the day when it would be all over. When the lease would be up. When she would be gone. When I could have my own life to myself at the end of June."

**What kind of pain did you experience?**

"It's incredibly painful," Justin said. "Everything about it. I didn't feel that she loved me anymore, or if she ever did. I thought I had found my lifelong soul mate. But I was wrong. And I was miserable. I *am* miserable. And so is she. She cries—a lot."

"It hurts to even talk about it," Brooke added. "I thought we were going to get married. If I hadn't thought so, I would never have lived with Justin. And now it's all over."

**Are you glad you lived together?**

"No," Justin exclaimed without hesitation. "Not at all. I would never do it again. And they say 'never say never,' but I think that given how painful it is now, the fact that a situation like this could come up again, I would never ever do it again. I would rather we made the financial sacrifice to set up two apartments so that the first day we lived together would be after our wedding! But living together when you're not married—not ever again. The next woman I live with is gonna be my *wife*."

Brooke thought for a moment before replying, "I really don't know if I would live with someone again. It hurts too much to even think about it right now. But I do know that I never want to experience this kind of pain again."

**What are some of the reasons that you would say "Never again"?**
Justin had made the original comment, so he responded:

> One reason is because look what happens after you break up and you still have to live together. Maybe some people have the funds where they can just move out, but normal everyday salt-of-the-earth people, when they sign a lease, they have to abide by it. And the breakup of two people is not something that you can just schedule. It will just happen. And sometimes it happens three or four months before the end of the lease. So then you have yourself in a situation that is completely horrible.
>
> I'm sure we're not the only couple that has found themselves living with their ex and things have gone horribly wrong—that's why they are your exes—yet the lease isn't up until whenever. So that has got to be the most horrible situation known to man. Well, actually I'm sure there are a lot worse situations. But that definitely deserves an honorable mention. So that would be the number one reason. But you don't realize that until after it all happens.
>
> The number two reason [has to do with love]. If you love the person wholeheartedly, then you should love them enough to marry them and then move in with them. If you're not sure it's the right person, don't do a trial marriage, which is really what living together is. It can lead to way too much pain.

And if you're assuming that you have found the right person, but you're just not yet ready for the wedding, don't move in together just to save money. Maybe that was the case for us, but because of our connection, I thought that she was the one. I really thought we were soul mates. And so I did think we were going to get married. But now it's obvious that we're not. If we hadn't moved in together, I still think we would have broken up before we made it to a wedding day, but we would have saved ourselves a lot of grief.

**If you were given the chance to stand up and talk to singles about living together, what would you say?**

Justin offered some advice:

I probably wouldn't approach it from a moral perspective. Today, everyone has his or her own level of morality. There's the Bible, and then there's everyone else's Bible. They all live to whatever they feel is right or wrong. Whether it's killing people or stealing candy. Wherever they personally draw the moral line. That is why some people justify moving in together and some people with an orthodox interpretation would not allow that ever, at all. So everyone has his or her own moral line. And starting off, I wouldn't even make it a moral argument.

From the standpoint of secular human beings, think about how bad it would be if you broke up. It's as simple as that. Because at the time you're thinking, *We're going to get married.* Or, *I think she's the one—my soul mate!* Or, *Hey, if it doesn't work out, we're not married, so the breakup won't be that bad.* Think again. You have a lease together, but it will not be that bad? Everybody's planning out your life together, but you still think it won't be that bad if you break it off? I would say, completely—morals and values aside—think of how bad *it would be* if you broke up.

Then after that, I'd make the argument that you shouldn't live together unless you're married. I think you can find out about someone—whether you want to marry that person or not—without having to live with him or her. You don't have to do a trial marriage by living together. That is a misconception that I would want to burst. Because once again, take away the morality of it, and just look at it from a completely secular standpoint. You can spend enough time with this person without having to move in with them. You can go over and stay at his or her apartment. And he or she can go over and stay at your townhome. It's kind of like living together, but then if she makes you mad, you can send her away. You know what I mean: Go to *your* home!

I would tell anyone who is thinking about living with someone else that there are plenty of ways you can spend time together to see if you are right for each other. You don't have to live together. In fact you shouldn't live together. Moving in together adds complications to the relationship that can lead to disaster. It's not worth the pain.

## NOT HAPPILY EVER AFTER

It had started out like a big-screen romantic comedy. Two people from totally different parts of the country meet each other, become friends and fall in love. They are soul mates. They start making plans for a life together.

Yet as I drove home after my conversation with Justin and Brooke, it was obvious that the ending of their story was far from "happily ever after." Instead, it was tragic, sad, painful. Two young people had scars that they will carry inside them for the rest of their lives.

Now would be a good time to stop and think. Think about what you have read so far. If you choose to live together before marriage, the odds of the two of you someday having a happy, successful, divorce-free marriage are not in your favor.

If living together is not a good way to prepare for marriage, then the question remains, How are two people who think they are in love with each other supposed to find out if they should get married? Should they just jump in and hope for the best? Or is there some other way to prepare for matrimony *and* avoid a divorce in the future?

The rest of this book will help you answer that question. There are actions that every couple can take before they make the big commitment. Although nothing can guarantee a divorce-free future, there are many ways to increase the potential for a long and fulfilling marriage.

PART 2

# How to Be Sure

C H A P T E R   5

# aRe you Ready?

Over the years I have performed a large number of wedding cer-
emonies—more than I can remember. Somewhere in the opening
of each ceremony I usually tell the couple's story: how they met,
how long they dated and what their first date was like. The highlight of the bride and bridegroom's story is often the description
of how he popped the big question.

I have heard my share of funny, serious, embarrassing and
heart-wrenching proposal stories. There have been rings in a

Cracker Jack box, romantic dinners on the beach and personalized billboards on a highway. Many times there has been meticulous planning leading up to the pivotal event.

I had my own beach experience more than 20 years ago when I asked my wife—then girlfriend—Bernice, to marry me. Bernice and I were spending the weekend in Monterey, California, with the college group from our church. Monterey is a cute coastal city with beautiful beaches. I knew this idyllic setting would be a perfect place to pop the big question, so I planned to ask her on Saturday.

Friday night Bernice and I drove to Monterey, a two-and-a-half-hour trip from our homes in Fresno. I will never forget that drive. My mind was going over my proposal plans. I was eager to get there.

On our drive to Monterey, Bernice and I played a cassette tape that someone had given us of a man they had heard on the radio. The speaker believed that Jesus Christ was going to return to Earth that very day, September 8, and take all Christians to heaven with Him. Because it was night and the day was just about over, Bernice and I were not putting much stock in his belief or teaching. But it was interesting!

As we drove and listened to the tape, I thought, *I sure hope this guy isn't right. I want to get married before I go to heaven!*

As soon as we reached the end of the tape, a bright fluorescent flash lit up a huge portion of the sky in front of us. It was so resplendent that we could see clouds that a second before had been hidden by the darkness of the night. We were both speechless as we stared up from behind the windshield. We had no idea what was happening. But our first thought was, *Wow, could this guy on the tape be right?*

We stared in silence as the light slowly faded to darkness. After a few seconds we looked at each other and said, "Well, we're still here!" The next day we found out that the light came from a rocket that had been fired from Vandenberg Air Force Base. That night I did not sleep well. My adrenaline was running high. With what Bernice and I had just experienced in the car, and my excitement about popping the big question, Saturday could not come soon enough.

> *The wedding ceremony is our society's way of separating those with strong emotions from those with also strong commitment.*
>
> TIM STAFFORD,
> WORTH THE WAIT

The next morning I awoke to a picture-perfect day. Bernice and I drove through Monterey. At one point, just as I had planned, we stopped at a beautiful spot overlooking the Pacific Ocean and I pulled out a letter that I had previously written. I told Bernice I had spent a lot of time thinking and praying about our relationship, and I wanted her to know how I felt. With that, I gave her the letter and asked her if she would read it. After she finished reading about my love for her and my desire to spend the rest of my life with her, I asked her if she would marry me. Obviously, as she is now my wife, she said yes.

## TWO KINDS OF COMMITMENT

I have done a lot of thinking, both before that day and since, about marriage commitments. What I have found is that the word "commitment" is at the heart of strong relationships. If at some point in your future you can see yourself popping the big question, commitment is something to which you will want to give some serious thought. Your commitment to commitment will have a direct bearing on the relationship you share with your future mate—and it will be the most important factor in divorce prevention.

The Bible has shaped most of my thoughts about commitment. Statistics—such as the ones presented in earlier chapters—actually support the principles I found there. In a nutshell, I have concluded that healthy marriages are built on *an unconditional commitment to an imperfect person by an imperfect person.* There are two kinds of commitment: conditional and unconditional. A conditional commitment is contractual. It is based on certain conditions being met or performed. If the conditions are not met, the commitment is null and void. An unconditional commitment is based on a covenant. No matter what happens, the commitment stands. It is not performance based.

**An Unconditional Pledge**
God designed marriage to be an unconditional covenant commitment—first to God and then between a man and a woman (see Mal. 2:14). The Bible suggests that a couple should seek to share the kind of commitment that God has with His children: unconditional and everlasting (see Ezek. 16:8,60).

In marriage, this commitment works best when the focus is on meeting each other's needs. The husband's commitment is to love his wife by nourishing and cherishing her. A wife demonstrates her commitment to love her husband by respectfully following his leadership (see Eph. 5:33). In the book of 1 Corinthians the mutuality of this sacrificial commitment is made clear. Paul writes:

> *It is only possible to live happily-ever-after on a day-to-day basis.*
> MARGARET BONANO

> The marriage bed must be a place of mutuality—the husband seeking to satisfy his wife, the wife seeking to satisfy her husband (7:3, *THE MESSAGE*).

As you can see from this passage that actually deals with sex within marriage, each partner should be focused on meeting the other's needs. This is never an easy task, but it is what makes a great marriage.

*Most married couples, even though they love each other very much in theory, tend to view each other in practice as large teeming flaw colonies, the result being that they get on each other's nerves and regularly erupt into vicious emotional shouting matches over such issues as toaster settings.*

DAVE BARRY

## The Power of Vows

A person with conditional commitment would, in essence, be saying, "I, John, take you, Mary, to be my wife as long as you keep me happy by cooking my meals, washing my clothes, meeting my sexual needs and paying the bills." Or, "I, Mary, take you, John, as my husband as long as you hold a well-paying job, mow the lawn, keep the cars washed and meet my emotional and relational needs." In other words, each takes the other for what he or she expects from the other.

The conditional partner says, "Because you will do something for me, I take you." This kind of commitment is based upon performance:

- I take you *to do*, not *to be*.
- If you are good enough, then I will love you now and keep loving you in the future—if you continue to meet my needs, my wants, my desires.

In contrast, unconditional commitment is symbolized in a wedding ceremony through the giving and receiving of vows. When each partner says, "I take you to be my wife (or husband)," an exclusive, relational covenant commitment is made. A good marriage is built upon an unconditional commitment in which each person focuses on meeting the needs of the other.

## Imperfect Partners

Every marriage commitment is made by an imperfect person to another imperfect person. Everyone comes into marriage with shortcomings. Your spouse *will* have flaws. As has been said before:

If you think you are marrying one who is *ideal*, do not be surprised if your marriage turns into an *ordeal*, which could make you believe your only way out is to get a *new deal*.

Unfortunately, in the world today more and more relationships that lead to marriage are based on conditional commitments. Prenuptial agreements are a perfect example of how this works. One partner or the other wants to protect his or her assets, reputation, feelings or other personal treasures *just in case it does not work out*. Therefore, a lawyer draws up a document that lays out the arrangement. This is not an unbreakable covenant; rather, it is a legally binding deal that specifies the consequences of one party or the other falling short—i.e., performance or lack thereof. In the case of celebrities Jennifer Lopez and Ben Affleck, it has been reported that she insisted he sign a prenuptial agreement under which he would pay her $1 million if he has an affair while they are married. How upside down is that?

> *We come to love not by finding a perfect person, but by learning to see an imperfect person perfectly.*
>
> ANONYMOUS

But the truth is, imperfect people cannot ever be good enough for long enough to sustain conditional, performance-based marriages. It is no wonder that the chances for divorce are twice as high among people who live together before marriage. Cohabitation sets a couple up for a performance-based relationship. When there are such conditions, the marriage usually does not last. If it does, the partners generally will be miserable.

## A Lifelong Promise

My wife and I have enjoyed marriage for more than 25 years. Fortunately, after I asked Bernice to marry me, we contacted a pastor who we knew could help us prepare for marriage. Our respect levels for Pastor Darryl and his wife were high and we wanted to glean what we could from him to get off to a strong start.

Darryl agreed to help us, and we made a commitment to get together with him several times during a three-month period. Although we had to drive more than 100 miles for our sessions with Darryl, our time with him was invaluable.

Of all the things that Darryl taught us, there was one principle that stood out. Although it was 25 years ago, I can still remember the session when Darryl looked lovingly into our eyes and said, "Dave, Bernice, you must make an unconditional commitment to love each other in your marriage."

Drawing a line in the air that vaguely resembled a roller coaster, he added, "Your marriage, if it is like most, will experience great highs and also deep lows, but you must not base your marriage on whatever emotions you feel at those times." Then he raised his hand again and continued, "Let the beginning of this line represent the commitment you are going to make to each other when you are married on January 10."

*Too many people marry for better or for worse, but not for good.*

ANONYMOUS

He continued his new line by purposefully drawing a straight horizontal line from left to right and said, "Your commitment should extend like this line from the day of your wedding ceremony until death do you part. When the low times come, make decisions based on your commitment to each other, not how you're feeling at the moment."

## NOW THE HARD PART

I have never forgotten Darryl's words. I am especially grateful that my wife has not forgotten them either. We have had our share of roller-coaster moments. We have enjoyed many times when life was wonderful—times when we were so thankful that we had chosen each other. But we have also had our share of low points in our marriage—times when life was not so great and nothing seemed to be going right. There have even been times when we were pretty frustrated and disappointed with each other.

Marriage is filled with ups and downs. But a stable, unconditional covenant commitment to love each other regardless of each other's shortcomings will get you through the lows. Making this commitment is the most important thing a couple can do to be sure that their marriage will last "for better, for worse—until death do us part."

*I once worked with a guy named George who, for Christmas, gave his wife, for her big gift—and I am not making this gift up—a chain saw. (As he later explained: "Hey, we NEEDED a chain saw.") Fortunately, the saw was not operational when his wife unwrapped it.*

DAVE BARRY

If you are trying to decide if you should get married, first ask yourself, *Am I ready to make an unconditional commitment to this person just as they are—for the rest of my life?*

## CHAPTER 6

# He Loves me, He Loves me Not

"I just want to be sure." The words came out of my mouth with a plea for help. I was sitting in the office of one of my closest friends. He knew me well. Of all people, Jim could help me sort out my feelings for Bernice.

Jim was 12 years older than me and had already gone through many of the things that I was now working through. At that point he had been married for eight years and had two children.

"So, Jim, what do you think? Should I marry her?"

Bernice and I had been dating for three years. I had completed college; she was in her last two years. I was 21; she was 20. I was in my first full-time job as a youth director. The income was not great, but it was not bad. I loved her. We enjoyed being together. She loved God. So did I.

As far as personality strengths and weaknesses were concerned, Bernice and I were different—very different! Where she was weak, in one or two places, I was strong. Where I was weak, in more places, she was much stronger.

So there I sat in the office of my close friend looking for direction in what I considered one of the most important decisions I would make in my life.

"Jim, what do you think I should do?"

I will never forget his answer. He leaned toward me and—with a tone of authority, confidence and excitement—said, "You'd be crazy *not* to marry her. Get with it!"

So, as you already know from reading the last chapter, I did.

## THREE KINDS OF LOVE

Many times over the past 25 years of my marriage and my ministry as a pastor, I have been the one who has been asked the questions: "Do you think we should get married?" "How can we know for sure?" "We don't want to end up divorced. How do we know if marriage will work for us?"

Should you get married? Here are some children's thoughts on the point:

- Just flip a nickel. Heads means you stay with him and tails means you try the next one. *Kelly, 9*
- You got to find somebody who likes the same stuff. If you like sports, she should like that you like sports—and

she should keep the chips and dip coming. *Allan, 10*
• No person really decides before they grow up who
they're going to marry. God decides it all way before,
and you got to find out later who you're stuck with.
*Kirsten, 10*

No one wants to end up "stuck with" a marriage partner.
The divorce statistics attest to that fact. But neither stuck nor
divorced are outcomes that God has in mind. Furthermore,
there is a better method for being sure than flipping a nickel *or*
trying each other out by living together before marriage.

It all comes down to whether two people love each other.
That may sound trite, but it rings true. Ask yourself, *Do we love
each other? Am I in love? Do I really know what it means to be in love?*

The Bible gives an inside look at love and marriage. Properly
understood, it can help two people decide if they have the kind
of love it takes to make a lifelong marriage commitment. The
Bible describes three kinds of love that are absolutely essential in
marriage and can help a person determine if he or she should
walk down the aisle.

### Eros: The Love of Attraction

I probably do not have to say much about this kind of love.
Physical attraction is not new. The Greeks referred to it as *eros*. It
has been a part of relationships for thousands of years. In fact,
you have probably been talking about it since you were an ado-
lescent. There have been many "hotties" to whom you have been
attracted. Am I right?

The Bible tells us about Jacob and Rachel's physical attraction for each other. She was "beautiful of form and face" (Gen.
29:17, *NASB*). In fact, the chemistry was so strong that Jacob was
willing to work for Rachel's father for 14 years in order to earn
the right to marry her! (See Genesis 29 for the whole story.)

A man and woman who are in love will have strong physical feelings for each other. It is a given. It is how men and women tick. But those feelings can get a person into a lot of trouble. The challenge is to keep physical attraction in check.

One of the strong indicators of whether or not you should get married is that you will be physically attracted to your partner. If you are not, you might want to take a step back and reevaluate your relationship. It is not that the other person has to be a hottie, but *something* has to be there. Some kind of physical chemistry must be drawing you together. You will either have that, or you will not. You will know.

Knowing this will spare you the pain that one woman had who wrote to advice columnist Ann Landers.

Dear Ann:

I have been married now for 12 years, but it is not a normal marriage. "Garth" has never—and I mean never—spent one night with me in the bedroom. We have had sex twice since our honeymoon, and nothing in the last 10 years. . . . The few times I have suggested intimacy, he yelled at me and threatened to move out. . . . Garth claims he loves me, but I'm not sure what that means anymore. . . . I am petite and attractive, and I have no idea why he isn't interested in me. Do you have any advice?[1]

Ann wrote back:

Sex is an integral part of marriage. . . . I hope you will go see a therapist immediately.[2]

Ann's right. God feels the same way. Unless there is some kind of physical ailment, physical love is vital in a couple's relationship. If there are no sparks between you and your partner, a bright yellow flag should go up. Pay attention. No one should have to end up like Garth and this attractive young woman.

### Phileo: The Love of Companionship

A second indicator to look for is the love of companionship. The Greeks called it *phileo*. Do you and your partner love each other from the depths of your beings? Are your hearts knit together? Is your soul in love with the one you want to marry? Do you have strong emotional feelings for each other? Is there tender affection between you two? Do you enjoy being together? Are you best friends?

The love of companionship is the love of friendship. The city of brotherly love, Philadelphia, gets its name from this form of love. The biblical characters Jonathan and David had this kind of brotherly affection for each other: "The soul of Jonathan was *knit* to the soul of David, and Jonathan *loved* him as himself."[3]

> *The bottom line is that we love each other, and what's more, we like each other.*
>
> PAUL MCCARTNEY, AFTER 29 YEARS OF MARRIAGE TO HIS LATE WIFE, LINDA

In the Bible the word "knit" is filled with meaning. Most often it is used to describe people who think alike—they have similar plans, goals, dreams or aspirations.[4] To be knit together is to be joined together.[5] These people are tied together.[6] They are leashed to each other.[7] They are bound to one another.

Common thinking, feelings, interests, likes, dislikes—you name it, they are as one. The bond between them is both emotional and experiential. When one rejoices, the other rejoices. When one hurts, the other hurts. This kind of love impacts their feelings. It may even result in tears. Jesus Himself wept for His friend Lazarus when he died. Jesus' tears over Lazarus's death prompted others to say, "See how He loved him!"[8]

When a couple shares this kind of love, even the thought of

the other's death, or of surviving after your soul mate dies, is devastating. When the sons of Jacob described their father's relationship with their youngest brother, Benjamin, they said Jacob's life "is closely bound up with the boy's life."[9]

Jacob's soul was one with Benjamin's soul. They went on to say that if Benjamin were to die, their father would also die.[10]

*Two souls with but a single thought, two hearts that beat as one.*

FREDRICH HALM

Brotherly love results in devotion.[11] This kind of friend loves at all times and sticks close to the other through the highs and lows of life.[12] At times such a love will require diligent effort. Even love between friends can be difficult at times, but it will grow as it is nourished.[13]

If someone asked you if you are in love, what would you say? If you felt phileo, your answer would likely be one of the following:

- "We're best friends."
- "We just love being together."
- "We have so much in common."
- "We like to do the same things."
- "We seem to know what each other is thinking."
- "Even when we're apart, we're not apart."

Before a couple marries, their souls need to be knit together in phileo. The more two people share in common in the depth of their beings, the better the chance of a successful marriage.

Think of it this way: If your soul were represented by one circle and your prospective spouse by another circle, there should be a lot of overlapping in your thinking, likes, dislikes, hopes, dreams, values, plans and more. If, however, there is very little overlapping, then your souls are not very connected. If that is the case, you'd better think long and hard about whether or not you should marry each other.

## Agape: The Love of Sacrifice

Strong marriages are built on sacrificial love. This kind of love requires an unconditional commitment and is described in 1 Corinthians 13:

> Love never gives up.
> Love cares more for others than for self.
> Love doesn't want what it doesn't have.
> Love doesn't strut,
> Doesn't have a swelled head,
> Doesn't force itself on others,
> Isn't always "me first,"
> Doesn't fly off the handle,
> Doesn't keep score of the sins of others,
> Doesn't revel when others grovel,
> Takes pleasure in the flowering of truth,
> Puts up with anything,
> Trusts God always,
> Always looks for the best,
> Never looks back,
> But keeps going to the end.
> Love never dies.[14]

That sounds like a huge commitment, doesn't it? It is. But that is exactly what it takes—commitment. A commitment to love the other person in spite of their imperfections, in spite of their failures and mistakes.

The Greeks called this kind of love *agape*. It is God's design that a husband love his wife sacrificially by nourishing and cherishing and honoring her.[15] A wife sacrificially loves her husband by respecting him and following his leadership.[16] Their relationship is based on mutual submission and sacrifice.

The epitome of agape is characterized by God's love for us. In one of the most familiar verses in the Bible we read, "For God so loved the world, that he gave his one and only Son, that whoever believes in him shall not perish but have eternal life."[17] This verse uses "agape" for "love." Personal sacrifice is at the heart of God's love for us, and it should be at the heart of the love we have for each other. "This is how we know what love is: Jesus Christ laid down his life for us. And we ought to lay down our lives for our brothers."[18]

*Some pray to marry the man they love, my prayer will somewhat vary: I humbly pray to heaven above that I love the man I marry.*

ANOUK AIMEE

When we sacrificially love, the focus is not on ourselves but on the other person. Most of us would like to think that we can pull ourselves together and love this way, but the fact is we usually do not. There are two primary reasons. First, this kind of love is foreign to our nature. Left to ourselves, our love usually comes out of selfish motives. Most love is motivated by what it can *get* as a result of acts of sacrifice. It works as long as there is a return on its investment. But when nothing comes back in kind, it feels used. It can give up.

The second reason why we may not love this way is because we do not have a personal relationship with

*You can give without loving, but you cannot love without giving.*

AMY CARMICHAEL

God. Unconditional sacrificial love ultimately comes from Him.[19] When God is invited to be Lord in a person's life, He releases His love in that person's heart.[20] He makes it possible for him or her to begin to love in ways that he or she previously would never have loved.[21]

Sustained, sacrificial love requires a spiritual connection to God. It is no wonder that God says the spiritual dimension is an important determining factor in whether or not a couple should marry. If a couple is not on the same page spiritually, they will lack the ability to grow in their sacrificial love for each other. And the god in their marriage will be someone or something other than the God who can give them the love they need.

*Love has nothing to do with what you are expecting to get, it's what you are expected to give—which is everything.*

ANONYMOUS

How will you know if the other person sacrificially loves you? How will he or she know if you love him or her? Here are a few things you should hear and see:

- Affirming and encouraging words
- A humble and forgiving spirit
- The desire to resolve conflict
- Patience and kindness
- Concern for your welfare and needs
- Humility—a willingness to admit wrong
- Self-control—not given to outbursts of anger or rage
- Attention—makes time to be with you
- Unselfishness—as able, buys things for you

Does the person you are considering marrying demonstrate sacrificial love toward you? Do you demonstrate this kind of love toward him or her? Are you willing to, or is something holding you back? This is not the kind of decision that you can "sort of" be sure about. You need to be completely sure.

## THE IMPORTANCE OF KNOWING

Several years ago my brother was married, but his marriage did not last. Neither I, nor anyone else who knew him, had any reason to think that he would ever end up getting a divorce. It was a shock to all of us. Before Greg, no one in our family had ever been divorced. We were fortunate.

But seven months after Greg and Becky's wedding, they severed the relationship. He and I have talked several times about what happened. Really it boils down to one thing: When he married, he was not absolutely sure she was the right one. But plans were in motion. Because he reasoned that doubts are normal, he went ahead with the nuptials.

Several things led to his uncertainty. For one, he had let his physical attraction (eros) for Becky get the best of him. He was too involved with her physically. That physical involvement, instead of adding to his certainty, actually hurt his certainty (I write more about this danger in chapter 11). As far as the other two areas of love go, they both fell way short.

Greg's most telling comment shortly after his divorce was "Even during our wedding ceremony, I knew I might be making a mistake—I just didn't know what to do about it at that point."

I made a commitment from that point on that I would do all I can to help couples be sure. Do not get married until you are absolutely sure. Do you love each other? I mean, do you *really* love each other? Is there a physical attraction? Are your souls knit together? Are you willing to sacrifice for this person? To what degree? Are you spiritually connected in such a way that God is causing you to love one another through sacrificial actions?

If you lack love in any of these areas, do not ignore your findings. It is not that the other person has to be perfect. That is not going to happen because none of us is perfect. But you need to look for some strong indicators that this kind of love is in your relationship and it is growing. Be sure!

CHAPTER 7

# What about sex?

My son Brian began driving at the age of 16—I mean on the very day he turned 16! Like most teenagers, he was eager to get his license and get out on the road—alone, or at least without his parents in the car with him.

Shortly after Brian started driving, he purchased his first car with money he had been saving. His mom and I liked the vehicle because it was a sturdy SUV. After the car was safety checked, Brian wasted no time getting out on the road—but not for long. Within four months he was in an accident and his car was totaled. After the accident Brian described for us how the whole thing happened.

> I had just merged onto the freeway and an old car pulled up in the lane next to me on my left. We drove side by side for a little ways, but then I remembered something you said to me once, "If a car or truck is driving right next to you, it's safer to either speed up, or slow down, and not keep driving side by side." So I let up on the gas and started to back off. And the second I did, that old car blew a tire. The driver lost control and his car spun into my lane and hit the front of my car as it flew by. His car ended up on the freeway shoulder with my car right behind his.[1]

Fortunately, Brian, his friend and the other driver all walked away from the accident without injury—it could have been a lot worse. Unfortunately, the whole thing happened because the other driver lost control.

The investigating police officer and the insurance company concluded the driver of the car that hit Brian was at fault. The final report said, "The loss of control was the result of negligence on the part of the car's owner. The tire that had blown, and the other three tires on the car were unsafe because they were bald."[2]

Automobile accidents often happen when a driver loses control. On Sunday, February 18, 2002, Dale Earnhardt, one of auto racing's greatest drivers, was killed on the last lap of the Daytona 500. He died when his out-of-control car hit a wall at 150 mph. Every year about 5,000 teenagers lose their lives in automobile accidents because they or someone else lose control.[3]

If you drive, someone in the past has probably told you, "Whatever you do, don't lose control. Drive with two hands on the steering wheel. Drive slower when you're in the rain. Slow down when you go around a corner. Just don't lose control." That is safe and sane advice—it probably came from someone who cares about your safety and future. That advice is not just for driving cars. It also applies to a relationship with someone of the opposite sex—do not lose control.

A lot of couples no longer feel the need to wait until marriage to have sex. Exercising sexual self-control is something of the past. "After all," they say, "what's wrong with sex outside of marriage? We love each other! We are sexually attracted to each other. We want to show each other our love."

# SEX: A GOOD THING

When God designed a man and a woman, He designed sex to be an enjoyable part of their relationship. His sexual design included sex within marriage. Without blushing, therefore, the Bible says:

The man and his wife were both naked, and they felt no shame.[4]

Honor marriage, and guard the sacredness of sexual intimacy between wife and husband.[5]

Enjoy the wife you married as a young man! Lovely as an angel, beautiful as a rose—don't ever quit taking delight in her body. Never take her love for granted![6]

Your stature is like that of the palm, and your breasts like clusters of fruit. I said, "I will climb the palm tree; I will take hold of its fruit."[7]

According to God, sex is a wonderful thing in marriage. Physical intimacy is something that God designed married couples to enjoy. God's not down on sex! He designed it. But sex with someone you're not married to spells trouble. That's why God says:

God wants you to live a pure life. Keep yourselves from sexual promiscuity.[8]

Don't allow love to turn into lust, setting off a downhill slide into sexual promiscuity.[9]

God draws a firm line against casual and illicit sex.[10]

We can't afford to waste a minute, must not squander these precious daylight hours in frivolity and indulgence, in sleeping around and dissipation.[11]

Why would God warn against sex outside of marriage? Because He is a prude? He's not with the times? Neither. Rather, it is because He cares about you. He loves you and wants what is best for your life—what will bring the greatest honor to Him as your creator.

## MAN AND WOMAN: CREATED FOR INTIMACY

Man and woman were created by God to enjoy intimacy—to be each other's companion. Aloneness was not good, so God designed man and woman to have relationship.

Physical intimacy was included in God's plan. He intended for a man and a woman to "become one flesh"[12]—but not with just anybody. The plan calls for only one person—the person you marry. Marriage is the only place where physical intimacy in all of its pleasure and emotional connection can be known. When it is removed from marriage, it will always be less than God desired and, ultimately, end in aloneness.

Your desire for intimacy can only be fulfilled in marriage. It is a big mistake to try to find it elsewhere. If you do try to find it elsewhere, you will experience false intimacy, which can set you up for relational and marital problems.

*You have to walk carefully in the beginning of love; the running across fields into your lover's arms can only come later when you're sure they won't laugh if you trip.*

JONATHAN CARROLL,
*OUTSIDE THE DOG MUSEUM*

## A Love That Fools

Sex outside of marriage can fool you into believing you have found the one you should marry. "Passionately in love" is not just a cute phrase. It accurately describes what a couple can feel for each other. You are physically attracted to each other and long to express that love sexually. Should you? God says no. If you do, you may be fooled into marrying the wrong person.

Of the three kinds of love discussed in chapter 6, sexual love (eros) will have the strongest impact on your feelings. It can easily sway you into thinking you are in love when it really may be just a strong physical attraction.

*Many a man in love with a dimple makes the mistake of marrying the whole girl.*

STEPHEN LEACOCK

A couple that engages in premarital sex may only be sexually in love (eros) and not realize phileo and agape are missing. With eros you feel close, because you are physically close. You feel pleasure, because there is pleasure. You feel love, because you are expressing love—physical love. But what you feel can mislead you. You can be easily deceived into thinking you are *in love*. Physical intimacy can fake you out!

The only way to keep your feelings in check before marriage is through sexual self-control. Do not fall for the adage, How can it be wrong when it feels so right? What feels so right may not be right for you. It may just be your hormones speaking. The best way to know who is right for you to marry is by exercising self-control.

### An Intimacy That Destroys

"Sex can be harmful to your health"—I doubt we will ever see an ad campaign with those words, unless it is referring to sexually transmitted diseases. But even the threat of disease is not enough to keep some out of bed. Getting a sexually transmitted disease may or may not happen. *After all, you may be thinking, those kinds of things happen to someone else.* Many people are willing to take the risk. But, aside from disease, there are inescapable consequences of premarital sex.

> *The truth is that whenever a man lies with a woman, there, whether they like it or not, a transcendental relation is set up between them which must be eternally enjoyed or eternally endured.*
>
> C. S. Lewis,
> *Screwtape Letters*

You are not just your body. You are body, soul and spirit. Sex outside of marriage is going to hurt you in all three areas. That is why the Bible warns against sex outside of marriage:

> The body is not meant for sexual immorality, but for the Lord, and the Lord for the body. Flee from sexual immorality. All other sins a man commits are outside his body, but he who sins sexually sins against his own body.[13]

> Abstain from sinful desires, which war against your soul.[14]

God wants to protect you from the destructive consequences of sex outside of marriage. Sexual immorality, though just one sin among many, is unique in that it will affect your body, soul and spirit like no other sin.

- **Body**—During sex, the most private part of your physical being is *joined* to another. Sex is the most intimate physical act that you can share with another person—and once you have committed the sexual act, you will never be able to get back your virginity.
- **Soul**—Through premarital sex, the innermost part of your being will sustain loss. A sacred part of who you are will be given away. You will be impacted emotionally—who you are in your innermost being. What you do with your body will have an impact on your conscience, commitments, values, personality, feelings, affections and desires. You cannot give your body away without giving away a part of your soul. The result often leads to feelings of having been used, being cheap and guilt.
- **Spirit**—Your relationship with God will be hurt. The sin in the act of premarital sex will block you from receiving God's best. He will be dishonored and His blessings will be impeded. God's desire is to fill you with love, joy, peace, patience, kindness, goodness, faithfulness, gentleness and self-control. But for Him to accomplish this work in you, you must be willing to live by His leading and not by the impulses of your flesh.

When I think about being out of control, I think of painful consequences, such as a car sliding off the side of an icy road, a hiker losing his footing and sliding down a steep hill or an unmarried couple giving in to sexual temptation.

I cannot see one advantage in losing control, but there are plenty of disadvantages. At the top of the list is how sexual immorality will affect your relationship with God, the very One you need to help you build a strong marriage.

## A Drive That Divides

Your sex drive may bring you together, but ultimately it may be the very thing that drives you apart. Even within marriage, sexual intimacy will not prevent a divorce, nor will it guarantee a long relationship. At its best, it may only keep the two of you together until someone better comes along.

As I was writing this chapter I received the sad but not unexpected news that another couple who had lived together had split up—after for four and a half years. She was having sex with another man. The guy did not see it coming and he was devastated. Now he is stuck living with the consequences. And he is ripped up inside.

# SEX: WHEN YOU REALLY WANT IT

Every unmarried couple I know struggles to restrain themselves sexually. Countless times I have heard singles say, "But I can't control myself." If that sounds like you, I have got the perfect answer: Get married! Soon. Really soon.

Marriage is a part of God's plan to help us place our sex lives under control. According to the Bible, it is better that a person marries than it is to live with burning sexual passion or to give in to sex outside of marriage.[15] So if you cannot wait for sex—get married.

## Self-Control

You say, "I'd love to get married. But I can't. Not yet. I'm still in school." Or, "I still haven't found the one. So what should I do *now*?" First, learn to control your body. Knowing the awful consequences connected to sex outside of marriage, the Bible gives this counsel, "It is God's will that you should be sanctified: that you should avoid sexual immorality; that each of you should learn to control his [or her] own body in a way that is holy and honorable."[16]

Self-control is something that must be learned. It will not come easily. It will not even seem natural. Your flesh will naturally want to give in to sexual desires. If you have found yourself tempted to give in to passionate urges, you are normal.

The late Dr. Curtis Mitchell, a former professor at Biola University, was speaking with a student once about what to do when tempted. The student said, "Well, Dr. Mitchell, we've already decided how we are going to handle it. We have a biology class together, so tonight we are going to gather algae off the rocks in Newport Beach. If we get down there and get tempted on that lonely beach, right on the spot we're going to kneel down and pray and ask God to help us fight this thing."

Dr. Mitchell said, "That's very pious, but that's very stupid!"[17]

Maintaining control, the Bible instructs, requires fleeing. We are never directed to *fight* sexual temptation; we are told to *flee* it.[18] This is what Joseph did when Potiphar's wife tried to seduce him. He did not suggest that they stop off at the couch, kneel and pray about it. He took off. In fact, he left so quickly that she was left holding his coat—and that led to big trouble for Joseph (see Genesis 39:7-20 for the full story).

Fleeing sexual temptation is an indispensable ingredient in controlling your body. It is something you must learn to do. And it is especially hard to do if you are living with someone of the opposite sex.

## God's Control

Restraint from sexual involvement is tough—really tough. I know. I was once in those shoes. So what do you do? You could just go ahead and have sex—or you could ask God to give you the strength to hold off on sex until marriage.

Fortunately God has not left us to struggle to maintain control all alone. He promises to give us the power necessary to live under control through the Holy Spirit. His plan is for His Spirit to completely control us. With the Holy Spirit in you, filling and controlling you, you will be able to keep your sex life under control.

The Bible likens the Holy Spirit's control to alcohol. It reads, "Don't be drunk with wine, because that will ruin your life. Instead, let the Holy Spirit fill and control you."[19] Live no longer under the control of wine, but be completely and always controlled by God's Spirit. Self-control is an indicator that God is controlling you.[20] Consistent self-control requires God's supernatural strength. We must learn how to receive His power and use it in this area of our lives.

*It was worth the wait.*

A. C. GREEN, RETIRED LOS ANGELES LAKERS STAR, FOLLOWING HIS HONEYMOON (HE ADVOCATES PREMARITAL ABSTINENCE AND DID NOT MARRY UNTIL HE WAS 38.)

## No Compromises

Some couples give in to sex by thinking, *At least we're not living together. It's better than the hundreds who are!* Or, *But we're planning on getting married.* The latter may be true, but we have already seen that a lot of people who are planning on getting married never do! And my desire is to encourage you to make a commitment to do what is best. Do what is going to give you the strongest foundation on which to build the rest of your married life.

## The Payoff

If you want to be sure that you have found the right mate, concentrate on building your relationship on emotional, relational and spiritual intimacy. Do not let your relationship get physical before marriage.

Because God loves you and cares about your welfare, He has set in place certain sexual limits. They are there for your protection. He wants you to live *under control* and avoid the inevitable hurt and loss that come to those who are living lives that are *out of control.*

The emotional, spiritual and physical oneness you long to experience as a couple is the by-product of waiting and marrying. "All in all," muses Harvard sociologist Christopher Jencks, "[adult premarital sex] may ultimately prove to be a little like smoking dope in the 1960s. In retrospect, maybe it isn't so good for you after all."[21]

CHAPTER 8

# 1-800-We-Need-Help

Toll-free numbers are popular around our house. We use them frequently—usually in a panic, when we desperately need help. If I am the one calling, it is usually after I have already wasted a lot of time and energy trying to make something work using my own limited knowledge or experience.

Lately, most of our 1-800 calls have been to our Internet provider. We are at the point where we no longer have to look up the number. We have called for help so many times that we can go through the maze of automated options without listening to the menu. We just punch in the right sequence of numbers and wait for a live voice.

At first I was reluctant to call our Internet provider. After all, with a little common sense, an ability to fiddle around and my experience I should have been able to solve just about any computer problem—not so. Once I made the call and got the help I needed, my lack of knowledge became obvious. The solution was simple, but I would have never figured it out on my own. I needed the help of someone more experienced than me. Help was available. All I had to do was make the call.

# THE NEED: HELP!

My golf swing is another not-so-classic example of what can happen to a person who thinks he or she needs no help. When I first started playing golf, I just went out with some friends and had fun. It did not seem like that big of a deal to swing the club and hit the ball.

*Unfortunately, most people spend more time preparing to get a driver's license than preparing for marriage!*

P. ROGER HILLERSTROM, *INTIMATE DECEPTION*

Today, I think you would call my swing adequate but far from great. It could be a whole lot better—if only I had asked for help from a professional right from the start. Now, after 25 years of playing golf, I have had pros help me many times, but it is pretty hard to undo the bad habits that I have already ingrained in my swing.

## A First Step

Would you classify yourself as reluctant or quick to get help? If you are feeling okay, but it is time for a physical, are you reluctant or eager to see a doctor? If your car starts making funny noises, are you reluctant or eager to take it to a mechanic? If you could not find a job, would you be reluctant or eager to ask a headhunter for some help? It all depends—right? You think, *Can*

*I do it myself, or is it something that requires professional help?*
I would like to convince you to get help before you get married. Do not make the mistake I made with my golf swing. Your marriage is far more important. Get some help now as individuals and as a couple from someone who knows what it is going to take to have a successful marriage. Shove reluctance as far away from you as possible, and eagerly embrace premarital help.

**A Search for Role Models**
If you are not sure you need help, take a brief look around you. Have you noticed how few marriage role models exist? How many couples do you know that have been married 25, 30 or 50 years? How many husbands and wives are happy in their marriages? Can you name even one couple you can point to and say, "I want my marriage to be like theirs"?

You probably have not seen many good marriages. Even the home you grew up in may have been broken. Or your parents' marriage may have been far from ideal. If you can relate to one of these scenarios, then you are not alone. Some authorities have suggested that only 1 out of 10 marriages could be classified as fulfilling or happy.

> *Personally I am always ready to learn, although I do not always like being taught.*
> WINSTON CHURCHILL

I firmly believe happiness in marriage is attainable. But with the way things are and the experiences most have gone through, outside help is needed. I urge you to embrace that help.

## THE QUESTION: WHO ME?

If you are still not sure you need help, you might want to think again about current divorce statistics. As I have noted, no one marries thinking he or she will ever divorce, but reality reveals some sad facts:

- 54 percent of American adults are married.
- 1 out of 2 couples that marries will divorce.
- 3 out of 4 couples that live together before marriage will divorce.
- 1 out of 4 adults has been divorced.
- Of the 2.4 million couples that marry each year, 400,000 of them will divorce within one year.

You and I know those statistics represent lives. Behind every divorce are broken dreams and broken people. Divorce hurts. And it hurts for life.

### Embrace Help

Marriage is too big a step to take without counsel. It is a wonderful commitment for two people to make, but before they do, they need to ensure that they are ready and that they gain every possible advantage so that they can end up on the positive side of divorce statistics.

*In the bakery department of a Dallas supermarket, a wedding cake was set out for shoppers with the sign: "He changed his mind. Have a piece of cake on us."*

FORTH WORTH
STAR-TELEGRAM

Not long before this book was written I received a phone call from an acquaintance named Heidi. She said, "I'd like you to help me and my fiancée, Jason, prepare for marriage. We haven't set the date yet, but we are thinking about sometime soon. Could you meet with us and help us make sure we're ready?"

Both Heidi and Jason are professionals in their respective fields. They are very intelligent, successful people. They are also wise. It was an honor for me to get her call. I was grateful not only for her respect of me as a pastor and person but also because she and her husband-to-be saw the need for outside help.

## Ask Questions

My sessions with this couple were similar to many others. From my training and 20 years of premarital counseling experience, I have learned that there are several areas upon which a couple should focus. If you plan to get married, I would urge you to consider working with someone who can help you talk about these issues:

- **Commitment**—What does a lifelong commitment entail? Are you ready to make one? Are you sure this is the person you can live with for life?
- **Expectations**—What do you expect and what will be expected of you? Are these expectations realistic?
- **Communication**—Can you build intimacy verbally?
- **Conflict**—This is a given in marriage. How will you handle it?
- **Personality differences**—How are you alike and different? What will this mean in your marriage?
- **Spiritual beliefs**—This is extremely important. Do you share the same faith and beliefs?
- **Roles**—Who will be responsible for what? How will decisions be made?
- **Sex and romance**—Are you ready emotionally and physically?
- **Needs**—We all have them. What are yours? What if your spouse stops meeting your needs?
- **Goals**—What hopes, dreams and plans do you have for your marriage? For your life? Does your spouse-to-be share those hopes, dreams and plans?
- **Finances**—Is budgeting important to you? Should it be? Do you have an adequate plan?
- **In-laws and friends**—What can you do to keep these on the asset side and off the deficit side of your lives?

- **Children**—Do you hope to have children? When? What things can you do to prepare for the challenging task of parenting?

## THE GUIDANCE: WISE VOICES

When I look at the above list of issues, I am reminded how on target the Bible is:

Where there is no guidance, the people fall, but in abundance of counselors there is victory.[1]

Without consultation, plans are frustrated, but with many counselors they succeed.[2]

For by wise guidance you will wage war, and in abundance of counselors there is victory.[3]

I do not mean to imply that marriage is war. That is not my, nor God's, idea for marriage. The point is, success and victory are connected to prudent counsel. Do not try to enter marriage without it. Ask for guidance from others who are wiser and more experienced than you.

The word "guidance" is a nautical term. It was used to describe the steering of a ship. Counsel can help you navigate the shallow or rough waters that may be up ahead. A counselor can help steer you in the right direction.

There are many places where you can get this kind of help. If you attend a church, you can ask there. Perhaps you have high respect for a married couple you know. Maybe they would be willing to meet with you and talk you through areas such as the ones listed above. You may want to meet with a marriage and family therapist or another trained counselor. You may know a teacher who would be willing to help. Perhaps your parents could lend some guidance. Draw from as many counselors as possible to help you prepare for marriage.

At least one of these counselors should be someone who is trained in dealing with marriage issues. He or she should possess the following qualities. You may not be able to find them all in one person, but I encourage you to look for as many of these qualities as possible:

*The truth is, married people of all income levels live happier, healthier and more financially stable lives than their single counterparts. The research on this is irrefutable. More than 30 years of studies have shown children raised in married-parent households fare much better than kids in any other circumstances. They are more likely to do well in school, graduate and go on to college. They are also much less likely to use drugs, engage in early sexual activity or commit crimes.*

FAMILY NEWS IN FOCUS

- Happily married
- Has been trained in premarital counseling
- Shares your spiritual beliefs
- Can administer a counseling questionnaire that will reveal possible strengths and weaknesses in your relationship with your spouse-to-be[4]
- Is willing to meet with you for more than one or two sessions (I prefer four to six)
- Will give you writing and reading assignments that will help you internalize and practice what you are learning

Are you ready to call for help yet? I hope so. But when you do, do not short-change the process by giving yourself too little time. I recommend not even setting a wedding date until at least midway through your counseling. That way you can be sure to take whatever time you need to adequately *be sure* you are ready for marriage.

# THE DECISION: WISE CHOICES

After a few counseling sessions, Heidi and Jason gave me an update on how they felt about their premarital counseling to that point. They said,

> This has been great. Better than we imagined. We are so glad that we are doing this. Before we started our sessions, after having dated now for two years, we thought we were ready. We felt like we had talked through everything we needed to talk about. But these sessions have helped us see more about our relationship. And it's been very revealing. We are so glad we called and asked for your help. It's already making a big difference and we can see how it will make a big difference in the future.

I agree with their assessment. When I look back on my own marriage, I am so glad for the premarital counseling Bernice and I received. It has made, to this day, a world of difference. Even after three years of dating, and as well as we knew each other, we still had our eyes opened to new things.

The pastor with whom we worked had us take several personality tests. One of them was meant to show us how well we knew each other. When the results came back, it was very clear that Bernice knew me really well. But the chart that showed how well I knew Bernice was a different story. Pastor Darryl had covered it with red lines and circles and the word "WHY?" written across the top of the page. Our discussion about that profile turned out to be one of the most helpful things I endured (I mean learned) through our premarital counseling.

# THE LAST WORD

Get guidance. It is worth it. Bernice and I are glad we did. Our marriage has been better for it. I have talked with numerous couples over the years who have said the same thing. In fact, I have never had a couple say to me that they regret the time they spent in premarital counseling. In fact, just the opposite is true: They are glad they made the 1-800-We-Need-Help call.

Whatever number you have to dial to get that help, do it. It will be one of the best investments of time you could make. And it will be the best way to help you decide if marriage is right for the two of you.

Now if I could only fix my golf swing!

PART 3

# Spiritual Insight

# CONSIDERING LIVING together

The first time Mark and Kathy met they knew there was something special between them, something that could lead to a lifelong relationship. "We immediately hit it off, " Mark recounted. "We met at an evening study group while we were going to college in Arizona. Some mutual friends, who had brought us to the meeting, introduced us."

"I liked what I saw," Kathy said. "And the few things we said to each other before the meeting made me think it would be fun to get to know Mark better." That opportunity came later that same night.

After the study group broke up for the evening, Mark and his brother, Doug, headed back home to the apartment they shared. A few minutes after they walked in the front door, Kathy's friend Nancy called to invite them out to get something to eat with them.

Having just finished a three-year stint overseas in the Army's airborne infantry, Mark was more than willing to get out on the town and have some good food and fun.

As Mark and Kathy got acquainted that first night at dinner, they realized they had a lot in common. Both had grown up in the Midwest. Mark had lived on a ranch, and Kathy's family had often visited relatives who lived on ranches. Both of them loved the outdoors. They enjoyed hiking and riding horses in the countryside. Both were attending college in Phoenix, Arizona. And like most college students, they were anxiously awaiting the day when they would graduate. Kathy had a year and a half left in her nursing program. Mark was completing his degree in history with the hope of one day teaching in a public school. He had at least two years of class work remaining before he would complete his current studies.

Though they had exchanged phone numbers, they did not talk to each other during the week after they met. They were just too busy with schoolwork. But they thought about each other and made sure they went to the Thursday-night study group again the following week.

After the Bible study, Mark and Kathy and Doug and Nancy had a quick bite to eat at Taco Bell and headed off for a late-night show—another fun evening. Kathy later said, "We had a great evening that night, but the highlight for me was when Mark asked me if I'd be interested in going out with him for dinner the next night.'"

Mark and Kathy's relationship progressed like that of many couples. They talked every day on the phone. They got together for coffee at Starbucks. They met each other's parents. They hiked several of the mountains in and around Phoenix. They ate a lot of dinners together and saw a lot of movies.

After dating for six months, they came to a place in their relationship where they were pretty sure they would get married someday—but not yet. They both wanted to finish college first. And that would take at least another year and a half.

Once they had come to this point in their relationship, Kathy suggested that they start living together. She thought that such an arrangement would be a great way for her to get out of her parents' home, where she was still living, and it would also be a good way to find out if Mark really was the one she wanted to marry.

In Kathy's family, living together before marriage was an accepted practice. Her mother and father had done it. So had two of her aunts and uncles. Even a few of her cousins were cohabiting—some with intentions of someday getting married, and others with no intention to ever marry. In addition, many of Kathy's close friends were already living with a boyfriend or girlfriend.

Kathy also had a pretty strong desire of her own to move in with Mark. "Mark and I talked about it all the time," she said. "We began to seriously consider it shortly after Mark's brother, Doug, had moved out. I can remember many evenings being alone with Mark at his apartment and I'd say to him, 'Mark, I don't want to go home. Can I stay? Let's live together.'"

Mark's background regarding living together was very different from Kathy's. Mark's parents had not lived together before marriage. None of his aunts and uncles ever lived together before marriage. And among his closest friends who were now married, none of them had lived together before they got married. So for Mark, living together would have broken the mold in his family.

## CHAPTER 9

# your most
# valuaBle asset

Many couples marry with a dream of one day building their own house. Have you had that hope? I did. I still do. My dream originated in high school in my favorite class: architecture. The year culminated with an assignment to draw, from scratch, our dream house.

For the project I had to draw up the floor and plot plans, including schemes for the foundation, electrical outlets, plumbing and roofing. The assignment also required that I design exterior color renderings and build a scaled-down, balsa-wood model of the house, including a removable roof that allowed us to look inside. The project took the entire year to complete, but it was a lot of fun and thrust me forward in what I thought would be my lifelong career.

I also took architectural classes during my first two years of college. What I learned from the professors gave me a great start in understanding the complexity and cost of building a house—especially a dream house. Houses do not just happen. They are the result of wisdom, planning, skill and a whole host of other important concerns. But when all these ingredients come together, someone's dream is realized and a beautiful house is built.

While in college, like many other students, my career path completely changed. In spite of my great love for architectural design, different doors began to open that eventually led me to where I am today. My love for building up people ultimately pulled me away from spending my life building houses. My last two years in college were spent preparing myself to be the best people builder that I could be.

I have been working now with singles and engaged people for more than 30 years. I do all I can to help them build their own dream house—not a physical structure, but a relationship. After all these years, I have discovered that my architecture background still comes in handy. Let me show you how a dream house is built.

## A QUALIFIED GENERAL CONTRACTOR

I have a friend who is a general contractor. Lee has been constructing houses for more than 50 years. I have seen his work—he is an outstanding builder. Without hesitation, I would recommend him. But as good as he is at building houses, I would never go to him for advice on how to lay the foundation of my marriage. He might have some good advice, but I know someone else who has greater skill and insight in this area. Of course, I refer to God.

A qualified general contractor has a crucial role in building a house. This person is responsible for the project, from start to finish. The task is huge. Everything from initial permit approvals to actual occupancy falls upon the general contractor's plate. Everyone looks to him, the expert, for the how, when and what.

### Shack Building

You can spare yourself a lot of hardship and sorrow by asking God to be the general contractor for your life and your marriage. From experience, I know that it will be one of the smartest decisions you will ever make. One modern paraphrase of an old proverb sums it up this way, "If God doesn't build the house, the builders only build shacks."[1]

I have seen shacks. I even had one in my backyard in California. We called it the toolshed. It started out being a fort for my two boys when they were younger. But after enduring years of pretend Indian attacks, make-believe guerrilla warfare and impossible missions, it was eventually just the place where we kept our lawn mower. It was missing boards and there were a lot of bugs and spiders—it was a shack.

### House Hunting

Couples house hunt. If you have not already done so, you probably will one day. You will get in your car or a realtor's car, and you will drive around town and look at houses. You will try to find one in which you want to live—one that is in the best location, fits your personality and is affordable. Some people think house hunting is fun. Others just want to get a roof over their heads.

For the purpose of my point, let's presume that after all your house hunting you have narrowed it down to two choices. You could live in a run-down shack or an executive mansion. Which would you choose? No doubt, all of us would want to move into the nicer place.

Occasionally a couple that I do not know wants me to marry them. One of the questions I always ask is, "Why do you want your wedding in a church?" Nine times out of 10 they say it is because they do not want to leave God out of their wedding ceremony or their marriage. I am glad. It would be a foolish thing to do.

So what does all this mean? Simply this: God is qualified to build your home. But you have to contract with Him to do that. If that is what you want, and I strongly suggest you should, then He is willing. But you must be willing to let Him have complete control. Are you willing to do that?

If not, it would be like building a home on your own and then inviting a master builder to your housewarming, expecting him to magically transform your shack into a dream house.

## A GOOD PLAN

Sarah Winchester's house epitomizes the let's-make-it-up-as-we-go-along building method. What began as an eight-room farmhouse in 1884, turned into a 38-year-long unfinished construction project. Mrs. Winchester had no master plan; instead, according to her carpenters, she built whenever, wherever and howsoever she pleased. At best, her planning consisted of occasionally sketching out individual rooms on paper and sometimes on tablecloths. No wonder she was constantly building, tearing down and remodeling her mansion right up to her death in 1922.

Sarah Winchester's 160-room house is filled with so many unexplained oddities, that it is now known as the Winchester Mystery House. Her Victorian mansion—complete with three elevators and 47 fireplaces—eventually engulfed several outlying structures on her 161-acre estate. Located in San Jose, California, this house is such an oddity it is now a tourist attraction. When you tour it, you find yourself saying, "What a waste!" It is totally random and makes no sense at all.

## Master Blueprint

It is not wise to build a home without a coherent plan. The results, as Sarah Winchester proved, are usually predictable. You waste time, effort and money. You can end up frustrated.

When it comes to marriage, the same principle holds true. Go forth without a plan and the result almost always is a fiasco. God wants to spare you from such a letdown. That is why He has provided a detailed plan on how to build a strong home.

The Bible is God's blueprint for home building. It recognizes that people need a solid and reliable plan. Proverbs is known as the book of wisdom. In it we read, "By wisdom a house is built, and through understanding it is established; through knowledge its rooms are filled with rare and beautiful treasures."[2] Jesus Himself later said,

> Therefore everyone who hears these words of mine and puts them into practice is like a wise man who built his house on the rock. The rain came down, the streams rose, and the winds blew and beat against that house; yet it did not fall, because it had its foundation on the rock. But everyone who hears these words of mine and does not put them into practice is like a foolish man who built his house on sand. The rain came down, the streams rose,

and the winds blew and beat against that house, and it fell with a great crash.[3]

Homes and marriages that withstand life's storms are built on God's eternal Word. The wise couple seeks not only to know what the Bible teaches but also to diligently apply it in their lives.

Advice, wisdom, training and many more things of concern are found in God's Word. I urge you to avail yourself of that help and to build your marriage on the principles that are offered to you in the Scriptures.

# A Solid Foundation

Any contractor will tell you that a strong house is built on a solid foundation. I saw this principle in action firsthand.

Southern California is notorious for earthquakes. Having resided here for 25 years, my wife and I have survived several. The worst one hit in 1994. That was the Northridge earthquake. Even though we lived 15 miles from the epicenter, our house and the houses surrounding us were all damaged—some just had minor cracks, but others were hit harder. Across the street, water heaters fell off their stands, broken glass was everywhere, and walls cracked. The damage on our side of the street was negligible. In our house, one saltshaker fell and broke, and the fireplace needed relatively modest repairs.

What made the difference? The construction of all our homes was the same—built on concrete slabs. All of the framing and joists were made of wood. The exterior and interior walls were covered with stucco and drywall. We all had composition roofs. But the one big difference was the ground on which our houses were built.

The houses on the other side of the street were built on fill dirt. Our lots were carved right out of the hillside and our homes built on cut dirt. In other words, all the houses across the street were built on a weaker foundation, so they shook like crazy when that earthquake hit.

*All weddings are happy.* At some point, an earthquake will
*It's living together afterwards* hit your marriage. But the good news is
*that is difficult.* that God has already provided a foun-
ANONYMOUS dation on which you can build your
home and it will enable your marriage to withstand whatever hardship comes your way. That foundation is Jesus Christ.

The Bible declares that Jesus Christ is "the living Stone . . . a chosen and precious cornerstone, and the one who trusts in him will never be put to shame."[4] This truth is invaluable in showing us how God offers us help through Jesus Christ:

1. **Jesus is a living stone.** He is not a dead, or lifeless, stone. These words, written after Christ's death, attest to His resurrection. He is alive, even though He died.
2. **Jesus is a chosen stone.** This imagery is taken from the Hebrew (Old Testament) Scriptures and shows us that the promised Messiah, chosen by God, would go to Zion (the city of Jerusalem) and sacrificially give Himself as an offering to save us from our sin.
3. **Jesus is a precious cornerstone.** Jesus' intrinsic worth and value beyond measure, as the most valuable stone in the building, stabilize and support the lives of all who build their lives on Him.

In ancient times, buildings were often made of stone. The cornerstone was the first laid and the most important stone in the building. It lay at the extreme corner of the building as an anchor. As the stone from which all measurements were taken, it made the foundation stable and the walls plumb and square.

The Bible describes Christ as our cornerstone. He is the One who gives us a solid foundation on which to build our lives. Of course, the question needs to be asked: Have you pushed Him over the hill? Are you building your life on Him? Everyone needs a cornerstone. Christ is that stone. And anyone who builds his or her life on Him, by faith is grounding that life on a sure foundation that will withstand every possible earthquake.

## THE SPIRIT WITHIN

The phrase "Don't leave home without it" is used to market a credit card. This card, the advertisements declare, is so valuable that wherever you go and whatever you do, you must have it with you. It can make your dreams come true. It can help you out when you are in trouble. Millions of people agree, so they say. Many of us listen, believe and carry one of these little plastic cards with us wherever we go.

God knew we would be in trouble if we tried to make a marriage work on our own efforts, so He made His help available every moment of every day through the work of His Spirit living within us.

The Bible shows us that the moment a person receives God's gift of life through Christ, God comes to live within him or her in Spirit form. When that happens to you, here is what you can expect:

1. **Encouragement and counsel**—Like a caring friend who comes alongside you, Jesus said the Holy Spirit will give this kind of needed help to each person.[5]
2. **Power and strength**—The same power that raised Jesus from the dead is the power that will give you strength to be all that God wants you to be.[6]

**3. Transformed character**—God's plan is to change you from the inside out so that you can grow to be strong in love, joy, peace, patience, kindness, goodness, faithfulness, gentleness and self-control.[7] Can you imagine the impact these qualities will have on your marriage and on the people around you?

All of this is possible to obtain through the work of God's Spirit inside of you. But there is a key to seeing God's Spirit impact your life and marriage in these ways. That key is your submission to God's plan and will for your life. You must be willing to walk in step with God, living under His leadership and allowing Him to change you from the inside out.

As you can see, it all comes back to this: You must want and seek God's help. You must ask Him to build your home. You must make Him the general contractor and willingly follow His plans.

Several years ago Dr. Nick Stinnett, the chairman of the department of human development at the University of Nebraska, placed an ad in 48 newspapers in 25 states. The ad read: "If you live in a strong family, please contact us. We know a lot about what makes families fail, we need to know more about what makes them succeed." Dr. Stinnett catalogued the responses into six basic elements. One of them was "Strong families have a spiritual commitment."[8]

> *A stronger marriage is a side effect of learning to love God.*
>
> ANONYMOUS

In an effort to draw on the wisdom of couples whose marriages where doing well, Dr. James Dobson polled 600 couples and asked them what concepts and methods have made the difference in their marriages. A Christ-centered home was first on the list. "Everything else rests on that foundation," the respondents said. "If a young husband and wife are deeply committed to Jesus Christ, they enjoy enormous advantages over the family with no spiritual dimension."[9]

These two studies have essentially concluded what I have been trying to communicate in this chapter. Couples who seek God's help will have stronger marriages. Make sure that God is at the very center of your marriage and your own personal life. Billy Graham was right when he said:

> Christ can transform your home. The tempers that have flared, the irritations that are evident, the unfaithfulness that is suspected, the monotony and boredom of existence without love can be changed and transformed by faith in Jesus Christ. . . . What Christ has done in other homes, He can do in yours if you will let Him.[10]

C H A P T E R    1 0

# tHe InstructionS

When it comes to following instructions, I would rather not. I am notorious for trying to do things my own way. Can you identify with that? I am a doer, not a reader. When I need to put something together, I dump everything out of the box and go for it, while the instructions sit on the floor—somewhere.

One time Bernice and I bought an inexpensive desk—the put-it-together-yourself kind of desk. It was very cheap. This one came with a bunch of pieces—I am not sure how many. I did not take the time to count them to see if they were all there, as I am certain the instructions would have told me to do. Instead, when

I dumped the pieces out of the box, there were boards and screws and who knows what all over the floor.

Like a good doer, I jumped right in. After about half an hour, Bernice came in and noticed that I had not even begun to put together anything even close to resembling a desk. And she could tell that I was frustrated. Knowing me well, she simply said, "You might try reading the instructions." Then she left.

She glanced back in the room a couple times shortly after that to see how I was doing. Each time, she saw that not much was happening, other than my frustration level rising.

The fact of the matter was, the more I tried to do it myself, the more annoying it became. The screws all looked alike. I would put two pieces together and then find out that I had to take them apart because I should have used a different piece. And each time I did it my way, I ended up stripping a screw or widening a hole so that when the correct screw was put into place, it did not fit right.

Finally, Bernice walked in, picked up the instructions and said, "Oh, look, Dave. There are all these cute little pictures that show you exactly how to put this thing together."

By this time, I was ready for help. But my mind quickly found a compromise, so I technically did not give in. "Okay," I said. "Why don't *you* look at the little pictures and tell me what to do!"

Not long after that we had a new desk and actually it is still holding up—probably because it is leaning against a wall. Thank God for instructions and loving wives who read them to their husbands.

## How to Know

The curious thing about instructions is there are *some* that even hardheads will not ignore. For example, one time I was home alone and made myself dinner. Before I took the chicken potpie out of the box, I read the instructions. Even I know it is too risky to cook without directions.

Would you attempt to fly without first signing up for instructions? The Federal Aviation Administration would certainly not permit that. You would probably kill yourself and be a danger to everyone else on the ground and in the sky. And you certainly would not want to board a plane if the pilot had not received proper instructions.

What about driving? I know one thing: We did not want our three kids driving without instruction. We signed them up for as many classes as we could get! Before any of us were ready to drive, we needed instructions.

You get the idea. Instructions are important. Actually, when you think about it, directions are needed for just about everything we do, even for marriage.

Fortunately, God has not left us to ourselves to try and figure out how to begin a relationship as husband and wife. I am sure He knew that when left to our own wits and desires, we mess it up.

## WHERE TO GET CLEAR INSTRUCTIONS

Some very important instructions on how to begin a marriage are found in the first book of the Bible:

> For this reason a man will leave his father and mother and be united to his wife, and they will become one flesh.[1]

These instructions are repeated in the Bible three more times.[2] When something is repeated three times in Scripture, it is because it matters a lot to God, and it should matter a lot to us.

In God's design, marriage should be entered into through the three acts of leaving, cleaving and becoming one flesh. First leave, then cleave and finally become. That is the sequential order God had in mind.

## Leave

*Leaving* will most often be signified by a public ceremony or wedding celebration. The word "leave" means to loosen, depart or abandon. It refers to leaving your parents— physically, emotionally and financially. It is getting out on your own.

## Cleave

The act of *cleaving* naturally follows leaving. The concept of cleaving can be signified in the personal commitment that each spouse-to-be makes to the other in the ceremony. To cleave is to glue something together. It is the welding of two pieces into one. Each is to be cemented to the other. An unbreakable union is entered into. This is where that unconditional commitment we talked about earlier comes into play.

*To read the Bible is to take a trip to a fair land where the spirit is strengthened and faith renewed.*

DWIGHT D. EISENHOWER

## Become

Following this unbreakable commitment, the couple is ready to *become* one flesh, to physically consummate their relationship, to join their names, to share a home and to build a new life together. After leaving and cleaving, the two become one.

# WHAT IS TYPICAL

The sequential order in a wedding ceremony and the subsequent honeymoon fit God's perfect design. Today, it is common at the beginning of the ceremony for the father of the bride to give his daughter away. This usually occurs after he escorts her down the aisle to the altar where her husband-to-be is anxiously waiting. The pastor asks, "Who gives this woman to be married to this man?" The father answers, "Her mother and I do." Then the father gives the bride a kiss and gently places her hand in that of the man who will now become her partner for life.

I once read about a wedding where five minutes before the ceremony was to begin, the father of the bride had still not shown up. After a frantic search they located him, still at home, and hurriedly got him to the church. They quickly began the ceremony. When it came time for him to answer, "Who gives this woman to be married?" he looked at the pastor and said, "Your wife and I"!

*A little girl at the wedding afterwards asked her mother why the bride changed her mind. "What do you mean?" responded her mother. "Well, she went down the aisle with one man and came back with another."*

ANONYMOUS

However the words come out, the intention on the part of the father is the same: to give his daughter away in marriage on behalf of himself and his wife. Publicly the bride has their support and permission to leave. A wedding ceremony serves as the defining moment when a couple begins a new life that is centered on the relationship that they share together, not around their parents.

The commitment to cleave to each other as husband and wife is wrapped up in the wedding vows that are exchanged during the ceremony. These vows reflect two people's desire to cleave to each other, to have and to hold from that day forward, for better and for worse, for richer and poorer, in sickness and in health, to love and to cherish, until death. A wedding vow should be an unbreakable commitment, before God and the witnesses present, that two people will be faithful to each other for the remainder of their lives.

Most couples follow their wedding ceremony with some kind of a reception and then get away for a much anticipated honeymoon, where the newlyweds experience the joy of becoming one flesh as husband and wife. This private consummation would naturally follow the public ceremony and personal vows of commitment. As husband and wife they join themselves together sexually. But this physical union is more than just a physical act. In the words of Clifford Penner, "This union encompasses the emotional, physical, and spiritual dimensions. Becoming one means joining all of who you are to each other."[3]

## HOW WEDDINGS HAVE BEEN DONE

We have come a long way from how weddings were done in Jewish families back in the days when the Bible was written. Historically, it was common on the day of the wedding for the groom and his friends, dressed in their finest clothes, to travel to the home of the bride. The bride, her family and her friends then went with the groom and his friends to what would soon be their new home. Exuberant singing and dancing would accompany this grand celebratory processional. Upon arrival at the groom's home, the couple was ushered inside the home where they physically consummated their marriage while the guests waited outside. Once they had officially become one flesh, the wedding festivities continued with a wedding feast. Often these celebrations continued for an entire week.[4]

Personally, I am glad that God did not prescribe how a wedding ceremony should be conducted. If I had my choice, I would choose our modern method over the traditional one! But I am glad that God gave us a sequential design for marriage that transcends time.

# WHY REDESIGN

God's original perfect order for marriage has been and is constantly being redesigned—not by God, but by people. His divine scheme has actually been reversed. Often, becoming is first and cleaving is last. Many people choose to begin a sexual relationship before they are married. The cleaving comes last, if at all.

> *In real love you want the other person's good. In romantic love you want the other person.*
>
> MARGARET ANDERSON

In 1969, a Gallup poll concluded that 68 percent of all adults and 49 percent of young adults believed premarital sex was wrong. By 1985, fewer than 20 years later, a Roper survey for *U.S. News and World Report* found that attitudes had flipped. The researchers concluded that 61 percent of all adults and 78 percent of young adults (ages 18-29) agree that premarital sex is acceptable.[5]

My heart went out to the young woman who wrote the following letter to Dr. Barbara Freedman:

> For as long as I can remember, my mother has told me that sex is something special and should be shared with someone you love. And believing her, I put up with all sorts of attitudes and jokes, because at the age of 22 I was still a virgin. Then I met someone I thought was terrific. We dated for four months before the thought of sex came up. We wanted to become friends before we jumped into something that serious. Nice guy . . . or so I thought. Then it happened. After a very romantic evening, we made love. Then he broke up with me. Several weeks later I found out he never cared about me at all. And that's not the worst of it. I just found out I'm eight weeks pregnant.[6]

Dr. Freedman wrote back:

> Lovemaking should not be taken frivolously as there are often consequences to this behavior—pregnancy being one.[7]

Tragically this young woman is also living with the hurt of having given herself and her virginity away to someone she thought loved her only to find out he did not. Her situation is duplicated thousands of times every day. Many people, however, have not given themselves to the one they love just once; rather, they do it many times—often in the context of living together. As with this woman, they eventually find out the hard way that physical consummation cannot guarantee a lifelong love relationship. Becoming has been ripped out of an unconditional commitment to cleave and conditionally inserted into noncommittal living together.

Today, although 90 percent of teens say they believe in marriage, 74 percent of them say they would live with someone before or instead of marriage. They reason, "If things don't work out, we can chalk it up to experience and move on. At least we will have learned something about ourselves and marriage."[8] This sounds good in

"Marriage" according to the dictionary:

1913: The act of marrying, or the state of being married; legal union of a man and woman for life, as husband and wife; wedlock; matrimony.[9]

1933: 1. The condition of being a husband or wife; the relation between married persons; spousehood; wedlock. 2. Entrance into wedlock; the action, or an act, of marrying; the ceremony or procedure by which two persons are made husband and wife.[10]

2000: 1. The legal union of a man and woman as husband and wife. 2. The state of being married; wedlock. 3. A common-law marriage. 4. A union between two persons having the customary but usually not the legal force of marriage: A same-sex marriage.[11]

theory, but as we have already seen, the results are usually far different from what people anticipate.

With intelligence and intention, God set certain laws into motion. It should not come as a surprise that when people violate these laws, situations often do not work out. Honestly, man's redesign for marriage is not a better design. Bluntly, it is worse.

If you are reading this book because you want to know how to best ensure a divorce-proof, happy marriage, a good place to start is by following God's instructions. Otherwise, you may end up as I did with my desk, putting the wrong pieces together first and becoming very frustrated. God's sequence was designed for the best results:

1. **Leave**—the public ceremony
2. **Cleave**—your personal commitment
3. **Become**—loving private consummation

CHAPTER 11

# PROTECT YOUR SOUL

Have you ever been in a tug-of-war? My most memorable tug-of-war was with a group of junior high students. At the time I was a volunteer staff member working at a junior high school in Fresno. Our Teen Dimension Club, along with 15 other clubs, had come together for Mud Day. I still do not know who came up with the idea, but it was pretty crazy.

Bus after bus brought in students for the big day. We all met at a ranch out in the country where staff members had worked for hours to create a huge mud hole. Actually, the hole was more

like a mud *lake*! Working with water trucks, fire hoses and trac-
tors we had come up with the perfect location and mud consis-
tency over which a giant tug-of-war would be waged.

The idea of a tug-of-war over a giant mud hole was not exactly
my idea of fun. I would have rather stood on the sidelines and
watched everyone else take a mud bath. But I was unable to find a
way out of the competition and was politely compelled to compete.
Suffice it to say that my team lost. To this day, I think I still have
mud in my nose and ears.

Every day we are all engaged in a big tug-of-war. The war is
being played out over a huge moral mud hole. I have found that
it is not an easy hole to stay out of, especially when it feels like
the opponents are stronger and have you outnumbered.

My son Brian got a firsthand taste of just how difficult it can
be on the underdog side of the big pull. Up until Brian's senior
year in high school, his beliefs about living together had not been
challenged in his classes. Then one day his English teacher
brought up the topic of a couple living together before marriage.
Brian told me it was a heated conversation that went on for more
than half of the two-hour class period. All 38 students, 19 boys
and 19 girls, had a strong opinion about people who live with
someone of the opposite gender before marriage. The over-
whelming majority said they planned to cohabit with any or all
prospective mates before marriage because they "need to be sure."

Brian and only one other student disagreed. They did their
best to argue counterpoints, even though they saw their opinion
falling on deaf ears. Often, those who are in the minority give in.
They go along with the crowd. They ignore the facts and what
they feel in their hearts.

In 1950, a psychologist named Ruth W. Berenda and her
associates carried out an experiment to determine how preteens
handle peer pressure. Groups of 10 adolescents were brought into
a room where the test was conducted. The test entailed showing

each group three separate charts, one at a time. On the charts were three lines. The students were to raise their hands when the teacher pointed to the longest line. What 1 person out of the 10 did not know was that nine of the others in the room had been instructed ahead of time to raise their hands when the teacher pointed to the second-longest line.

1. _____
2. _____
3. _____

Inevitably, when the nine raised their hands to vote for the wrong line, the odd-person-out would glance around, frown in confusion and then slip his or her hand up, thus joining the group. The test would continue after a brief reminder of the instruction to vote for the longest line and then the next card would be displayed. The researchers found that each time the student would end up voting for the second-longest line rather than go against the majority opinion of the group. This astonishing conformity occurred in about 75 percent of the groups of adolescents. Berenda concluded that "some people would rather be alike than right."[1]

The word "conformed" conveys the idea of taking on an outward form. It is to assume an outward expression that does not come from within. When I conform, I masquerade. I playact. I put on a mask in order to hide what is beneath. The outside is not congruent with what is on the inside.

The real you is inside you. God made you with a mind, a will and emotions. You have a heart, a soul and a conscience. If you follow Christ, you also have God's Spirit, the Holy Spirit, living inside.

What is inside of you is going to be tested by what happens around you. It will be challenged by what other people think and feel. It will be measured against how others live. Your response will either put you in the mud or keep you out. You will know when you are close to falling in, because your conscience will work to keep you from what could be harmful to your life.

God sends warning messages to us through our conscience. These messages are intended to protect us and keep us out of harm's way. The conscience is an innate ability, placed in us by God, to give us a sense of right and wrong. Our conscience will prompt us to do what is right and restrain us from doing what is wrong. When we violate our conscience, it will condemn us and trigger feelings of shame, anguish, regret, anxiety, disgrace and fear. When we follow our conscience, it will commend us and bring joy, serenity, self-respect, a sense of well-being and gladness.

*In our society, "conscience" has been replaced by "feelings."*

ANONYMOUS

I have been a counselor for many years and have discovered that deep down most people know it is better to marry before living with a romantic partner. This conclusion often comes out of their convictions and values. It also is often connected to God prodding their conscience to do what is best.

The Bible informs us that there is a war that is continually being waged for our soul.[2] The world around us is trying to pull us down and get us to give in to what our body desires and to what those around us are doing.

Our soul, which is referred to as our heart, is our inner moral nature. If the world can get into our soul, it can do great damage. It is no wonder that the Scriptures declare, "Above all else, guard your heart, for it is the wellspring of life."[3] Life flows from our heart and soul. Whatever we do, we need to protect our soul in the same way we would protect drinking water.

Most of us do not have to personally concern ourselves with protecting our water supply. We trust someone else to do that for us. But if we had our own well, we would do whatever was necessary to ensure we had clean, fresh drinking water. We would keep it free of sewer water. We would not allow children to swim in it. Our clothes would be washed somewhere else. Why? Because drinking water is necessary for life. It is that simple.

Take care of your heart. Take care of your soul. Do not give in to your sexual urges before marriage. Shrug off others' advice to live together as a couple before marriage. Your target should be to live with a *blameless, clear, clean* conscience. Hitting that target will keep your life and faith from a shipwreck.[4] To do otherwise will result in being pulled into the world's mud hole which could result in a *seared* conscience, a *wounded* conscience or a *defiled* conscience.[5]

> *There is an eagle in me that wants to soar, and there is a hippopotamus in me that wants to wallow in the mud.*
>
> CARL SANDBERG

Sometime ago I read about a 16-year-old girl who came in to see her pastor. She was in complete despair. She was struggling with the aftermath of having sex outside of marriage. She had not looked in a mirror for months, because she could not stand to see herself. To the pastor she looked nearer to 40 than 16. She was on the verge of suicide, not wanting to live another day. That day, that pastor had the joy of helping her start her life over through faith in Jesus Christ. Afterwards she said, "For the first time in years, I feel clean."

For your own good, hold yourself back. Do not give in. It will be worth it. It will not be easy, but you will be better off if you do.

I have long admired now-retired basketball star A. C. Green. At the age of 36 he had not married and was still a virgin. In an interview sometime ago he said, "I am still a virgin. Abstaining from extramarital sex is one of the most unpopular things a person can do, much less talk about it. From a sheer numbers standpoint, it can be a lonely cause—but that doesn't mean it's not

right. I abstain as an adult for the same reasons I did as a teen—
the principle doesn't change, or the feeling of self-respect I get."[6]

Self-respect is a feeling that comes from within when your
conscience agrees with your conduct. You will feel good about
yourself and you will maintain respect in the eyes of others.

The only way to have a clear conscience is to heed the inner
prompting of God. Determine to never do something that
would violate your conscience. Live a life that is above reproach.

> George Washington had it right when he wrote his
> college-age nephew:  A good moral character is the first
> essential in a man. . . . The habits contracted at your age
> are generally indelible, and your conduct here may
> stamp your character through life. It is therefore highly
> important that you should endeavor not only to be
> learned but virtuous. . . . You must know that without
> [virtue] you can never be qualified to render service to
> your country.[7]

With all of the soccer teams I have worked with throughout
the past 14 years, a number of people in the community have
come to know that I am a pastor. That has its advantages and its
disadvantages. One of those advantages came when a soccer couple was referred to me. They were looking for a pastor to do their
upcoming wedding.

We hit it off well from the moment we met. Their love for
Christ and each other made it a joy for me to help them prepare
for their wedding. We spent many hours together talking about
their hopes and dreams. Our premarital sessions focused on
strengthening their relationship with each other and with God.
We focused on vital topics such as communication, finances,
roles, love, expectations, needs, in-laws, conflict resolution and
sexual intimacy.

In the course of our premarital counseling sessions, we talked about their commitment to wait until marriage to live together. This personal pledge was made even though both of them had friends who were living together or had lived together before marriage.

Travis and Nicole wanted to follow their consciences. And they wanted their lives to please God, who had given them consciences. They wanted to have a positive impact on the soccer community, too. I am glad to say they did. On the day of their wedding, when they stood on the beautifully decorated platform in the church with their groomsmen and bridesmaids—all soccer players—they stood out because they had not given in. Everyone on the platform and in the audience watched with admiration and respect. There were no regrets.

## LISTEN TO YOUR INNER VOICE

In 1984, an Avianca Airlines jet crashed in Spain. Investigators studying the accident made an eerie discovery. The cockpit recorder revealed that several minutes before impact a shrill, computer-synthesized voice from the plane's automatic warning system told the crew repeatedly in English, "Pull up! Pull up!" The pilot, evidently thinking the system was malfunctioning, snapped, "Shut up!" and switched the system off. Minutes later the plane plowed into the side of a mountain. Everyone on board died.

Do not make the same mistake by ignoring the voice of your conscience. Protect your soul by doing what you know is the right and the best thing to do. Stay out of the mud.

## CHAPTER 12

# tHe View fRom aBove

Tyler and Tammy sat in my office. "We've been living together for the past six years and now we would like to get married," Tyler said. "Will you marry us?" I am asked that a lot these days. The question is not new. What is new is *when* it is being asked. Now the question usually comes after a couple declares, "We've been living together."

This time, "Will you marry us?" was being asked by a couple I had never met before. Tyler and Tammy had been given my name by a relative whose son I had coached in baseball some years ago. Our first contact was on the phone when the groom-to-be called to see if I was available to do a July 15 wedding, a date three months away. The date was clear on my calendar, so I suggested that we get together to talk about it.

We had a fun time getting to know each other. Tyler was 30; Tammy was 25. Neither of them had been married before. Both had stable jobs. He worked at a talk-radio station in the Los Angeles area. Five nights a week he did a three-hour, call-in show. As I got to know him, it was obvious that being a talk-show host fit him well. He had a great voice and was articulate, well read and more than willing to tell me how he felt about everything from marriage to politics to church.

The bride-to-be had an attractive personality and presence. Tammy had rapidly moved up the corporate ladder in an international travel and vacation company. Working at her full-time job, along with finishing cosmetic college and preparing for the wedding, kept her very busy.

After we got acquainted, I asked them to tell me about the spiritual part of their lives. I wanted to know if there was a connection between that and wanting me as a pastor to perform their wedding. They considered themselves to be Christians but were not active in a local church. They wanted their wedding ceremony to be done before God with His blessing. At one time the prospective groom had been preparing for full-time ministry. The bride-to-be had gone to a private Christian elementary school. They both wanted God to be at home in their home and hoped to one day return to a local church.

As our conversation turned toward spiritual matters, I asked, "Why, as professing Christians, did you decide to live together outside of marriage?" Tammy replied first, "Before I could ever think of marrying him, I needed to live with him to see if we were compatible. Now I know we are." Tyler nodded in agreement, adding, "Why not? After all, the Bible doesn't come right out and say that it's something a couple shouldn't do. In fact, didn't Mary and Joseph live together before marriage?"

## GOD'S POINT OF VIEW

Even among many Christians today, living together before marriage is not only permissible, but some also consider it a good thing to do. A few, such as Tyler and Tammy, even maintain that it is biblically justifiable. Not long ago I met with a professing Christian who feels that living together is acceptable "as long as you are planning on getting married." Is it? What does the Bible actually teach?

Let's consider these questions in light of two New Testament stories. In the first story, Jesus had a significant encounter with a Samaritan woman. Jesus had stopped with his disciples to rest at Jacob's well. A woman from a nearby town was also there—she had come to draw water. Jesus asked her for a drink and then offered her something: living water. She presumed He was talking about literal water, which would make future trips to the well unnecessary.[1]

*We sleep together. I love the idea of him holding me in his arms and loving me. I thank God for sending me a companion.*

ANONYMOUS 87-YEAR-OLD SINGLE WOMAN. HER MATE IS 90.

Jesus' offer, however, was spiritual in nature. He wanted to give her water for her soul. But before He could give the gift, she had to see her real need, which was not well water but salvation from a life of sin.

Jesus told the woman to go get her husband and bring him to the well. She replied that she had no husband. Jesus already knew that—and more—so Jesus said, "You have well said, 'I have no husband'; for you have had five husbands, and the one whom you now have is not your husband."[2] Jesus' reply was forthright and straight to the point. This woman was not married to the person with whom she lived. And prior to her current living arrangement, she had been married and divorced five times.

This woman was apparently living in sin. In Jesus' mind, living together outside of marriage was sin. She needed to see that what she was doing was contrary to God's will.

Dr. Laura Schlessinger is known for having a strong stance on morality and marriage. One person wrote this letter to Dr. Schlessinger:

> I have been dating the man I am currently engaged to for about three years. We are getting married next year. Last year, we bought our first home. Prior to this, we both lived at home with our parents: I am 24, and he is 26. We moved into the house and had a housewarming party. My mother told my future mother-in-law and later me that she felt it was inappropriate for us to have an open house before we were officially married. I feel bad for disappointing my mother. However, my fiancé and I are both excited about our new life together and our new home. We will be married very soon. We both have good jobs, college degrees and worship in church every Sunday. I dedicate three hours a week to singing in the church choir, and I feel I am a good person with great moral judgment. Do you think our judgment was out of line when we chose to move in together and have a party?[3]

Dr. Laura pulled no punches in her reply:

> Yes. Has something changed or does the church not condone shacking up or fornication? When you say you are a member of the church, does that not mean that you define "moral" by the divine authority of God's law—and not what is just exciting at the moment?[4]

Dr. Laura has hit the nail on the head: Living together, even with plans to be married, still does not make it moral or right.

# THE WAY THINGS WERE

Joseph and Mary stand out as a couple who did it right when it came to the matter of living together before marriage. A Jewish marriage was entered into in three steps.

The first step could be called the *family contract*. At the time of Christ's birth, parents arranged marriages. Contracts were made between two families. In ancient Jewish life, the parents chose the mates for their children. Although romance before marriage was not unknown in Old Testament times, it played a minor role in the life of those who married. They did not marry the person they loved; they learned to love the person they married.

Finalizing a marriage in ancient times began with the son's father agreeing on a price to be given to the father of the girl. The payment was compensation for the loss of a worker. After this agreement was made, the couple was considered engaged.

An engagement, or betrothal period, was a binding agreement that set the young woman apart for the young man. The agreement could only be broken by death or divorce. The length of engagement varied. Sometimes the couple was married the same day they were engaged. Usually, however, a period of time elapsed between the betrothal and the marriage ceremony. During this time the young man prepared a place in his father's house for his bride, while the bride prepared herself for married life. The betrothed couple would not live together, nor would they engage in sex.

A family contract was followed by a *public announcement*. The couple's engagement would be announced to others. This event was usually followed by a year of waiting before marriage. The waiting period was to demonstrate the faithfulness of the bride's purity. If she was found to be with child in this period, she would be considered impure, as one who had been involved in an illicit sexual relationship. Such was grounds for an annulment. This was precisely what Joseph was planning to do when Mary was found to be with child during his engagement to her.[5] If a bride was found to be pure throughout the engagement period, a wedding ceremony would follow.

*Warning: This book (the Bible) is habit-forming. Regular use causes loss of anxiety, decreased appetite for lying, cheating, stealing, hating. Symptoms: increased sensations of love, peace, joy, compassion.*

ANONYMOUS

The *wedding ceremony* was the third and final step in a couple's marriage. This was a huge event that was celebrated over the course of an entire week. It was not until after the ceremony that a couple would finally begin to live together as husband and wife.

The story of the woman at the well and the story of Mary and Joseph stand in stark contrast to each other. One could be yours.

The woman at the well was living with a man and they were engaged in a sexual relationship. Mary and Joseph, though engaged to be married, were not living together and had not engaged in premarital sex.

The woman at the well was living in sin. On the other hand, Mary was described as "favored" and "blessed," while Joseph was called "a righteous man."[6]

The woman at the well had disregarded God's way for her way. Mary and Joseph were committed to the rules of engagement and marriage God's way.

How about you?

# WE CHOSE NOT TO LIVE TOGETHER

Before I asked Bernice to marry me, our dating experience had been similar to most and we were ready to move on to greater intimacy. We had known each other for six years. We had been dating for three. I had just completed college. Bernice was beginning her junior year in college. Both of us had lived the previous two years away from home in Santa Barbara in separate dorms at the same school.

The summer after I graduated, Bernice and I moved back to our hometown where I worked full-time and she completed her last two years of college. She was 20; I was 21. Yes, we were both young, but we felt that we were ready to move past dating and into a deeper commitment. We were at the place where many couples today, perhaps even you, consider living together. We could have done the same. After all, we loved each other and we were planning on getting married.

Why not? Neither one of us wanted to move back home, having already been out on our own. And it would have made more sense financially to share the cost of one apartment than pay to live in two separate homes.

Yet Bernice and I never really seriously considered living together. Our personal convictions, the cultural circumstances of the time and our parents no doubt influenced our decision. I admit, at that time 25 years ago, it was not only almost unheard of but also frowned upon to live with someone of the opposite sex without being married. "Good" people just did not do that sort of thing! But more important, our personal spiritual convictions gave us even stronger reasons for why we wanted to get married before we lived together.

Not long ago I helped another young couple, Mark and Rachel, prepare for marriage. If I could choose a couple I would encourage others to learn from, it would be this one. They are committed to pleasing God both individually and as a couple, in everything they say and do.

The three of us talked candidly about their premarital commitments. Even with their wedding only three months away, they remained committed to waiting until marriage to have sex and live together.

Early in their counseling I asked them why they did not just move in together. They said they could not as followers of Christ. They believe that God's desire is for them to wait until they are married. They want the world to see Christ in them. And they want their testimony for Christ to be unmarred.

If you are a person with spiritual beliefs, I challenge you to take a stand for what God says is right.

## CHAPTER 13

# the perfect wedding

Weddings come in all shapes and sizes. My wife and I had ours in the First Baptist Church of Fresno. It is a big church with beautiful stained-glass windows. There was never even a question about where we would be married. We both had grown up attending that church. Our families were members. Most of our friends went there. And I was a staff member there! Eloping to Las Vegas was not an option.

So we had a church wedding at *our* church. The only question was how many of our pastors we could work in to the ceremony.

We ended up with three tying the knot real tight and a big choir singing from the balcony. There were a bunch of witnesses, too, just in case we ever woke up and wondered if the whole thing had really happened.

Regardless of where your wedding is held or how many people come, a wedding should be a day of celebration. Such was the case for King Solomon and his bride. I believe it can be the same for you. The same four things that made their wedding a perfect celebration will add to your celebration as well.

# 1. CELEBRATE WITH YOUR FAMILY AND FRIENDS

By virtue of not living together before marriage, your wedding day will be a celebration. After all the days, weeks, months or years of dating, you will have a lot to celebrate. Your parents have probably prayed for this day for years. Your friends who wondered if this day would ever come, will naturally be excited for you. And you will both be so glad it has finally arrived. After all the prayers, preparation and patience, you should celebrate—not just as a couple, but also with all those who have supported you and helped you get to this day in your lives.

Here's a glimpse of Solomon and his bride's wedding. It was a huge celebration.

Who is this coming up from the desert like a column of smoke, perfumed with myrrh and incense made from all the spices of the merchant? Look! It is Solomon's carriage, escorted by sixty warriors, the noblest of Israel, all of them wearing the sword, all experienced in battle, each with his sword at his side, prepared for the terrors of the night. King Solomon made for himself the carriage; he made it of wood from Lebanon. Its posts he made of silver, its base of gold. Its seat was upholstered with purple, its interior lovingly inlaid by the daughters of Jerusalem. Come out, you daughters of Zion, and look at King Solomon wearing the crown, the crown with which his mother crowned him on the day of his wedding, the day his heart rejoiced.[1]

At first glance, their wedding seems rather peculiar with columns of smoke, warriors with swords, purple seats and a mother crowning her son. Totally unfamiliar stuff to us. But a closer look at their ceremony that happened 3,000 years ago actually reveals several traditions that are still found in today's weddings.

Solomon's wedding began with a processional, as most weddings do today. But his was a little different. Then, all eyes were fixed on Solomon as he came for his bride. Today, all eyes are fixed on the bride as she walks down the aisle to her groom.

*Dartmouth University estimates that a good marriage is worth $100,000 a year. It came to this figure by adding what we would spend on other things to be equally happy without marrying.*

TIME MAGAZINE

Solomon's processional was a public event. He came across the desert accompanied by clouds of myrrh, frankincense and scented powders. Everyone living in the surrounding area came to watch. Today the bride usually arrives at the beginning of a by-invitation-only event in a dust-free church or ballroom with rose petals strewn on a white walkway.

Solomon was accompanied by 60 of his best men. Each one dressed in full military uniform with swords. Today there might be five or six best men, each one dressed in a rented tuxedo. Solomon's best men were there to do more than just keep him from backing out. They were there to ensure the safety of Solomon and his bride while they traveled across the desert. Today the groom's best men are usually close friends or family and are there to add their support and enjoy the fun.

Solomon's 60 men surrounded a special couch limousine that transported him and his bride-to-be to the wedding. A group of women from Jerusalem had decked the couch out. It was no doubt the best traveling couch in the land, made out of the best wood and overlaid with the most expensive materials available—silver, gold and purple fabric. Today a couple usually rides after the wedding in a limousine or a special car that is often decorated with shoe polish, streamers and tin cans.

> *The highest happiness on Earth is in marriage. Every man who is happily married is a successful man even if he has failed in everything else.*
>
> WILLIAM LYON PHELPS

Like most weddings, Solomon's was well attended. A number of women from Israel had come to share the joy of this day. Solomon's mother, Bathsheba, was there. She crowned him with a garland wreath, which signified her love and approval. His father, David, evidently had already died, so she alone was left to let Solomon go as he left home to cleave to his lovely wife. To this day weddings are well attended. Family members and friends come to share in the joy and excitement. But in contrast to Solomon's day, the bride is usually the one given away by her father.

Solomon's wedding was *the day his heart rejoiced.* His heart had longed for this day. When the day finally arrived, he and his bride-to-be were filled with joy. Contrary to those who poke fun at couples that marry, weddings are joy-filled occasions. Let the celebration begin.

When King Solomon married, he and his bride had not lived together. They had followed God's plan and that added to their celebration. Had they lived together before marriage, their wedding day would have been a lot different. Their wedding would have been more like a birthday than a birth.

# THE EXHILARATION OF BIRTH

Birthdays can be a lot of fun. They celebrate another year of life. But birthday parties in no way compare to the celebratory feelings new parents, and their families and friends, have at the birth of a child.

At a birth, the level of anticipation and excitement is off the chart. Hearts are filled with joy. The parents cannot contain themselves. They call all of their family and friends. And their family and friends call all of their family and friends. Dads take one picture after another and then speed off to the one-hour photo place to get the pictures developed so that they can start showing them to everyone. Some record the birth on videotape (I am not sure I would want to ever see that video). Others send out digital pictures via e-mail. Everyone who hears about it wants to share in the parents' joy.

A wedding can be like a birthday or a birth. When a couple lives together before marriage, their wedding is more like a birthday. Everyone is happy for you. They want you to have a lot of fun. But a birthday is not as exciting as a birth—just like a wedding after a couple has lived together is not as exciting as the wedding of a couple who has not lived together.

## Weddings in Contrast

| Have already lived together | Haven't already lived together |
|---|---|
| After the fact | Before the fact |
| Acknowledgment | Anticipation |
| Old news | News |
| Not a big deal | A big deal |
| Mild happiness | Intense excitement |

## 2. Pure Unadulterated Love

When I perform weddings, I get an up-close and personal view of the couple. From my vantage point, I like to watch a couple's eyes. Once while the groom was repeating his marriage vows, I actually stopped him. He was looking at me instead of at his bride-to-be. I suggested he look into *her* eyes, instead of mine, and make his commitment to her.

It was a pretty funny moment in the ceremony.

Couples can say a lot to each other through their eyes. Without saying a word, their eyes can express

> *Marrying for love may be a bit risky, but it is so honest that God can't help but smile on it.*
>
> JOSH BILLINGS

their love. Tenderness, compassion, concern, commitment and sexual interest can all be expressed through the eyes. When loving eyes and loving words are combined during the wedding ceremony, it is a sacred moment.

Solomon and his bride shared their love for each other through their eyes and their words. I would have loved to be there to hear his words when he said to her:

> How beautiful you are, my darling! Oh, how beautiful! Your eyes behind your veil are doves.... Your lips are like a scarlet ribbon; your mouth is lovely. . . . Your two breasts are like two fawns, like twin fawns of a gazelle that browse among the lilies.... All beautiful you are, my darling; there is no flaw in you. . . . You have stolen my heart, my sister, my bride; you have stolen my heart with one glance of your eyes. . . . Your lips drop sweetness as the honeycomb, my bride; milk and honey are under your tongue.[2]

Here is what she said to him:

Awake, north wind, and come, south wind! Blow on my garden, that its fragrance may spread abroad. Let my lover come into his garden and taste its choice fruits.[3]

This was a beautiful moment for Solomon and his bride. Having waited to live together, and to have sex, they now unashamedly expressed the depth of their feelings for each other. Today, we would say "They are madly in love with one another."

*I look forward to the day I can look my husband in the face and say, "I loved you before I even knew you. I saved myself just for you."*

LAKITA GARTH

And they were able to look into each other's eyes and express the depth of that love. He told her how beautiful she was to him—how she had stolen his heart, how he longed to show her his affection and love. She in turn invited him with poetic beauty to possess her, consummate the marriage and, at long last, share sexual intimacy.

Just imagine experiencing this kind of a moment on your wedding day. Picture looking into one another's eyes and expressing from the depth of your hearts your unadulterated love for each other. This kind of experience should actually happen. It can happen.

The choice will be yours. But when you express your vows to each other, I hope your moment will be like Solomon's. You'll be able to look each other in the eyes and express that depth of your love. And that love will come out of a heart of purity and passion. You will be caught up in the moment. You will say what you mean and mean what you say.

## 3. THE EXHILARATION OF SEXUAL INTIMACY

Once the ceremony was completed, Solomon and his bride were overcome with sexual desire for each other. Now at last, as God intended it to be, as a married couple, Solomon lovingly invited her to share sexual intimacy with him. She, in turn, invited him for the first time to share sexual intimacy with her. Afterward, Solomon said:

> I have come into my garden, my sister, my bride; I have gathered my myrrh with my spice. I have eaten my honeycomb and my honey; I have drunk my wine and my milk.[4]

Sexual intimacy, for Solomon, was like gathering myrrh in a garden. It was as sweet as eating honey, as enjoyable as drinking the best wine and milk.

Their wedding night was as beautiful, intimate and fulfilling as God intended it to be. They had nothing of which to be ashamed. They had every reason to enjoy giving each other pleasure. Unselfishness prevailed. Romance and affection abounded. Both of them greatly enjoyed the experience. It was good. They had become one flesh, just as God had intended.

*In a great romance, each person plays a part the other really likes.*
ELIZABETH ASHLEY

Dannah Gresh had this kind of experience on her wedding night. She wrote:

> I lay with my body wedged between my new husband's, amazed at the gift of our first experience together. It was tender, fulfilling, proof of our love. It was awkward and unperfected, proof of our innocence. Never, in all of my life, had I felt this warm and comforted as if the world had stopped around me simply so that I could really know and feel this moment.
>
> Bob began to move away from me. "No, don't go," I murmured, drawing him back to me. He turned and

kissed me tenderly on the nose, then proceeded to get out of bed. He tenderly and tightly wrapped me in the blankets and then knelt beside me. "Dannah, I want to pray," he said. "I want to thank God for this gift and beg his blessing upon our marriage bed that we might always protect it." There in the night with the moonlight shining a ray of light across our honeymoon bed, we praised the great God of the universe for our wedding night.[5]

This couple's story, like that of Solomon and his bride, can be yours. And it will be yours, if you wait until marriage to share yourself sexually with each other.

## 4. GOD'S ENTHUSIASTIC APPROVAL

At the end of Solomon and his bride's wedding day, God spoke—not to chastise or to correct, but to affirm what they as a couple had experienced:

Eat, O friends, and drink; drink your fill, O lovers.[6]

Not only did God approve of their wedding and sexual intimacy, but He also told them to enjoy the latter as if it were a banquet—that is how He planned it to be for a husband and wife.

I cannot think of anything better than hearing at the end of your wedding day God adding His stamp of approval and also encouraging you to live it up.

If you are willing to wait until marriage to begin living together, you are going to reap huge dividends. You will know the joy and happiness that come from having waited. Your ceremony will be filled with anticipation and excitement. Your guests will celebrate with you. Your love for each other will ooze out of your eyes and words.

Mike and Gail are doing it right this time. Mike has been married before. He tied the knot after he and his girlfriend had been sexually involved for a number of years. That marriage ended in divorce after he caught her sleeping with another man. She left him. He spent years trying to put the marriage back together, but it never happened. Now he is living in the painful aftermath. His failed marriage is still sucking energy out of his life. His 10-year-old daughter is hurting, too. She is shuttled every week between Mike and his first wife, who now lives 350 miles away.

> *Those who love deeply never grow old; they may die of old age, but they die young.*
>
> LADIES' HOME JOURNAL

Gail has never been married, but she lived with a man and had a child out of wedlock. For years she has lived as a single mom with one income from her full-time administrative assistant job. She has struggled to make ends meet for herself and her 13-year-old son. Each day, it has been early to rise and late to bed. Her son's love of soccer has kept her busy in what little free time she might otherwise have to rest. She has been making it, but it has been rough. Really tough!

Mike and Gail both know what it is like to live together before marriage. They would never do it that way again. This time, with God at the center of their lives, they waited. Waited to have sex. Waited to live together.

Do Mike and Gail have any regrets this time? Not one. Are they glad they waited? You bet. They know firsthand from failed experience why it is better to marry before you live together.

When Mike and Gail got married, their ceremony was a celebration—a perfect celebration. It was not perfect because everything was perfectly planned and all the right guests came. What made it special was what their wedding represented. It was the culmination of their dating and engagement. Their family and friends were there. It was something that they had longed for and anticipated. Their love for each other was expressed through their words and eyes. Then, finally, they no doubt sexually consummated their marriage while on their honeymoon. God is looking down on them with pleasure.

Make your wedding a celebration. Marry before you live together.

# mark and kathy: the Decision

Mark and Kathy had many long discussions about whether they should live together or not. Ultimately, they decided against it for three primary reasons.

Mark and Kathy sought out a respected pastor to help them begin to work through their feelings for each other. In the course of these appointments they began to discover that God's plan is for a couple to marry before they live together. That was news to Kathy. As a new Christian she had never heard this information before. As she was growing up, she assumed that God pretty much left it up to each individual to decide what would be best for him or her. Now she realized that God has given us in the Bible guidelines for living. And those plans are still relevant today. Once she discovered that, she knew it would be better to wait until marriage before she lived with Mark.

Mark's personal spiritual commitments also kept him from agreeing to living with Kathy before marriage. Mark said, "God designed a certain order to things—one being that a couple should live together after marriage and not before."

Statistical information that Mark had read also kept him from giving in to living with Kathy. "I read a lot," Mark said. "I had read several articles about studies that had shown that couples who live together before marriage have a greater likelihood of not staying together. In fact, they were more likely to eventually get divorced! If you look at living together from a statistical point of view, you are more likely not to succeed. And those who do live together end up with a lot more problems."

The experiences of others also helped convince Mark and Kathy not to live together. "Talk about problems," Kathy chimed in. "Since Mark and I started talking about whether we should live together, I've had a few heart-to-heart conversations with my aunt. She's been pretty candid with me. She actually admitted that if she had it to do all over again, she would never have lived with her husband before they got married. In fact, she said they probably wouldn't have ended up getting married if they hadn't lived together. And that would have been just fine with her, because today she's miserable. They lived together because it seemed like the right thing to do. Then they got married because it seemed like the next thing to do. And 11 years later, they're just existing together."

"Then," Kathy went on to add, "my mother and father are also on my firsthand bad-experience list. I hate to say this, but their marriage is in the pits. It has been for a long time. As far as I can tell, if they based their decision to marry on their living-together experience, they should have never done either."

The look in Kathy's eyes told me she was really hurting for her parents and her aunt. And that she did not want that kind of life for herself and Mark.

"So," I asked, "if your spiritual commitments, statistical data and others' experiences led you to conclude that living together wasn't such a good idea, how were you going to know for sure if you should marry each other?"

"We worked on that by focusing on building a strong relationship with each other with God's help," Mark replied.

Kathy added, "We had a really good relationship. We were happy. We got along really well. We learned how to work through our misunderstandings."

"We worked really hard to get to know each other better," Mark added. "We spent a lot of time together just talking."

"And we talked about everything! But especially our relationship," Kathy said. "We often talked about where we had been. The things we were learning about each other and ourselves. We talked about the changes we could see in each other. The ways we were growing. Our hopes and dreams.

"And we learned to forgive. When you spend a lot of time together, things come up. And we tried not to ignore issues. When we said something stupid to each other, we tried not to sweep it under the carpet. But we tried to address it in a spirit of love and truth wrapped in forgiveness."

"We had our difficulties and struggles. Everyone does," Mark said. "But the amazing thing is our love for each other grew in spite of our shortcomings and failures. And we learned to accept each other for who we really are, faults and all."

"What about sex?" I asked. "Did you have a commitment to be sexually pure until marriage?"

"Yes, we did," Kathy answered. "And that was especially difficult for Mark."

"Yeah," Mark replied. "It was not easy. And I definitely discovered that God did not make me to be single! But in spite of the temptations, I wanted to keep things pure in our relationship because I knew that sex was something that happens only for a moment. And it can deceive you into thinking that you have something between the two of you, when all you really have is something physical for the moment. I wanted a relationship that would last and stand the test of time. That's why I was willing to wait for sex until we married. Until then I wanted to do all I could to keep building a strong relationship between the two of us in other areas."

"So it sounds like you're glad you chose not to live together," I concluded.

"We are really glad." Kathy said. "We decided that we wanted what's best. We wanted to be sure. And now we're even more convinced the best way to be sure is by waiting to live together until after we marry. I used to think otherwise, but now I am convinced this is the best way to go. And as far as we can see from here, the way our relationship went, and the help we got from the two counselors at our church, confirmed our strong desire to marry each other."

"We could hardly wait to live together," Mark replied, "but we were willing to wait. It was just going to make our wedding and marriage all that more special. Not only for ourselves, but also for our family and friends—especially Kathy's family and friends. They were watching us like a hawk! They really wanted to see this work out for us. And we prayed it would. We believed with God's help we would be married some day and hopefully be a positive example of what God had in mind when He designed marriage."

Mark and Kathy both looked up. Mark said, "Dave, if others asked us for advice on living together, we'd say, 'Don't live together before marriage; it will cause more problems than it will solve.'"

After Mark and Kathy married, they moved in together. Doug and Nancy (who are also now married) were in their wedding party. A celebration? It was a celebration unlike any wedding celebration that had gone before in Kathy's family.

Regrets? None.

Happiness? Yes.

Perfection? No.

But Mark and Kathy prepared for living with their imperfections while dating, while they lived apart. And today, with God's help, their strong, loving marriage is a testimony to their family and friends of the benefits of waiting for marriage before living together.

# YOUR STORY

One of the main reasons couples decide to live together is so they can find out if they are compatible before they make the commitment to marry. They assume it is the best way to ensure a divorce-free future.

But the statistics show that living together before marriage actually increases the chance of getting a divorce.

There are other alternatives to living together that can help you determine if you should get married. They will do a better job of helping you make that decision. And if you decide that you should not get married, you will be able to move on with much less pain and emotional scarring.

- Seriously consider whether you are ready and willing to make an unconditional commitment to an imperfect person.
- Take time to discover if you love each other.

  Eros—physical attraction

  Phileo—friendship, common interests, companionship, shared values

  Agape—sacrificial love, putting each other's interests above your own

- Don't get involved sexually. Physical intimacy will mess up your perspective.
- Seek counsel of others.

Justin and Brooke's story, and many others like theirs, are great examples of the excitement that can lead to living together and the pain and regret that are all too often the consequences of living together. My hope for you is that you'll be spared that kind of pain.

If you are thinking about living with someone, I urge you to think long and hard about it and then base your decision on the facts and God's counsel. Don't settle for what others say or what seems like a good idea. Remember, the facts prove that if you choose to live together, the odds of living happily ever after are not in your favor.

The best chance for a happy ending to *your* story does not lie in living together. Rather, take the time to get to know each other without the complications of living together. Seek outside help in determining if this really is the one for you. And when you find that person and are willing to commit yourself to each other for the rest of your lives, get married and then live together.

# endnotes

## Chapter 1

1. As of November 2002, Arizona, Florida, Idaho, Michigan, Mississippi, New Mexico, North Carolina and Virginia have laws (that are rarely enforced) that make unmarried cohabitation illegal.
2. "No Comment Zone," *World Magazine*, April 15, 2000. http://www.worldmag.com/world/issue/04-15-00/opening_2.asp (accessed March 28, 2003).
3. Bureau of the Census, *Statistical Abstract of the United States: 1997*, prepared by the Bureau of the Census (Washington, D.C., 2000).
4. Ibid.
5. Larry Bumpass, "What's Happening to the Family? Interactions Between Demographic and Institutional Change: Presidential Address, Annual Meeting of the Population Association of America," *Demography*, vol. 27 (1990), pp. 483-498.
6. Pamela J. Smock, "Living Together: Facts, Myths, About 'Living in Sin' Studied," (speech presented at University of Michigan, Institute for Social Research, February 4, 2000).
7. Ibid.
8. Terry A. Lugaila, "Marital Status and Living Arrangements: March 1998 (Update)." Census Bureau Report, March 1998.
9. "Where's Daddy? . . . And Who Cares?" *World Magazine* (September 12, 1998), p. 10.
10. Bureau of the Census, *Statistical Abstract of the United States: 1997*, prepared by the Bureau of the Census (Washington, D.C., 2000).
11. Bureau of the Census, *Unmarried Couple Households by Presence of Children: 1960-Present*, prepared by the Bureau of the Census, (Washington, D.C., June 29, 2001).
12. Larry Bumpass, James A. Sweet, and Andrew Cherlin, "The Role of Cohabitation in Declining Rates of Marriage," *Journal of Marriage and the Family*, vol. 53 (November 1991), pp. 913-927.
13. Bureau of the Census, *Statistical Abstract of the United States: 1996*, prepared by the Bureau of the Census (Washington, D.C., 1996).
14. "Help for the Professional," *All About Cohabiting Before Marriage*. http://members.aol.com/ cohabiting/res1.htm (accessed March 2002).

15. George Barna, "Born Again Adults Less Likely to Co-Habit, Just as Likely to Divorce," news release from Barna Research Group, August 6, 2001.

## Chapter 2

1. Harriet Lerner, "Good Advice," *Harriet Lerner, Ph.D., Clinical Psychologist and Author.* http://www.harrietlerner.com (accessed April 2002).
2. Robin Fields, "Unwed Partners Up 72 Percent in U.S.," *Los Angeles Times* (August 20, 2001), p. 1.
3. Kit Russell, quoted in "The Pastor's Weekly Briefing," *Focus on the Family,* vol. 9, no. 24 (June 15, 2001), n.p.
4. Roland H. Johnson III, "Cohabitation: Good for Him, Not for Her" (1996). http://personalwebs.myriad.net/roland/cohab1.htm (accessed March 22, 2003).

## Chapter 3

1. Alan Booth and David Johnson, "Premarital Cohabitation and Marital Success," *Journal of Family Issues* (1988), pp. 261-270.
2. T. R. Balakrishnan et al., "A Hazard Model of the Corvariates of Marriage Dissolution in Canada," *Demography,* vol. 24 (1987), pp. 395-406.
3. Neil Bennett, Ann Klimas Blanc, and David E. Bloom, "Commitment and the Modern Union: Assessing the Link Between Cohabitation and Subsequent Marital Instability," *American Sociological Review,* vol. 53 (1988), pp. 127-138.
4. James A. Sweet and Larry L. Bumpass, "Waves 1 and 2: Data Description and Documentation," *A National Survey of Families and Households,* February 13, 2003. http://www.ssc.wisc.edu/nsfh/home.htm (accessed March 31, 2003).
5. "New Report Sheds Light on Trends and Patterns in Marriage, Divorce, and Cohabitation," *National Center for Health Statistics,* July 24, 2002. http://www.cdc.gov/nchs/releases/02news/div_mar_cohab.htm (accessed March 31, 2003).
6. Scott M. Stanley and Howard Markman, *Marriage in the '90s: A Nationwide Random Phone Survey* (Denver, CO: Prep, 1997), n.p.
7. David Whitman, "The Trouble With Premarital Sex," *U.S. News and World Report* (May 19, 1997), pp. 57-64.
8. David R. Hall and John Z. Zhao, "Cohabitation and Divorce in Canada," *Journal of Marriage and the Family* (May 1995), pp. 421-427.
9. Jan Stets, "Cohabitating and Marital Aggression: The Role of Social Isolation," *Journal of Marriage and the Family,* vol. 53 (1991), p. 670.

10. Susan L. Brown and Alan Both, "Cohabitation Versus Marriage: A Comparison of Relationship Quality," *Journal of Marriage and the Family*, vol. 58 (1996), pp. 668-678.

11. Catherine Cohan, quoted in Carin Gorrell, "Live-in and Learn," *Psychology Today*, November/December 2000. http://www.psychologytoday.com/ htdocs/prod/ptoarticle/pto-20001101-000012.asp (accessed March 31, 2003).

12. Ibid.

13. Chuck Colson, "Trial Marriages on Trial: Why They Don't Work," *Breakpoint* (March 20, 1995), n.p.

14. Jan E. Stets and Murray A. Straus, "The Marriage License as a Hitting License: A Comparison of Assaults in Dating, Cohabitating, and Married Couples," *Journal of Family Violence*, vol. 41 (1989), p. 39.

15. "Bureau of Justice Statistics," *U.S. Department of Justice.* http:// www.ojp. usdoj.gov/bjs/abstract/cv73_95.htm (accessed April 4, 2003).

16. Jessie Shirley Bernard, *The Future of Marriage* (New York: World Publishing Company, 1972), n.p.

17. Steven L. Nock, "A Comparison of Marriages and Cohabiting Relationships," *Journal of Family Issues*, vol. 16 (January 1995), pp. 53-76.

18. Robert Schoen and Robin M. Weinick, "Partner Choice in Marriages and Cohabitations," *Journal of Marriage and the Family*, vol. 55 (1993), pp. 408-414.

19. J. D. Cunningham and J. K. Antill, *Under-Studied Relationships: Off the Beaten Track*, vol. 6 of *Understanding Relationship Processes* (Thousand Oaks, CA: Sage Publications, 1995), pp. 148-172.

20  "A Few Facts on Cohabitation," *All About Cohabiting Before Marriage*, July 1999. http://members.aol.com/cohabiting/facts.htm (accessed March 31, 2003).

21. Ibid.

22. Edward Laumann et al., *The Social Organization of Sexuality: Sexual Practices in the United States* (Chicago: University of Chicago Press, 1994), n.p.

23. Alfred DeMaris and Gerald R. Leslie, "Cohabitation with the Future Spouse: Its Influence Upon Marital Satisfaction and Communication," *Journal of Marriage and the Family*, vol. 46 (February 1984), pp. 77-84.

24. Joyce Brothers, quoted in K. C. Scott, "Mom, I Want to Live with My Boyfriend," *Reader's Digest* (February 1994), pp. 77-78.

25. "What's Sex Got to Do with It?" *Michigan Family Forum* (1998), n.p.

26. Renata Forste and Koray Tanfer, "Sexual Exclusivity Among Dating, Cohabitating and Married Women," *Journal of Marriage and the Family*, vol. 58 (1996), p. 33.

27. Laumann et al., *Social Organization of Sexuality*, n.p.

28. Scott M. Stanley and Howard Markman, *Marriage in the '90s: A Nationwide Random Phone Survey* (Denver, CO: Prep, 1997), n.p.

29. "Sociological Reasons," *All About Cohabiting Before Marriage*, July 1999. http://members.aol.com/cohabiting/soc.htm (accessed April 1, 2003).

30. Susan L. Brown and Alan Booth, "Cohabitation Versus Marriage: A Comparison of Relationship Quality," *Journal of Marriage and the Family*, vol. 58 (1996), pp. 668-678.

31. Larry L. Bumpass and James A. Sweet, "National Estimates of Cohabitation," *Demography*, vol. 26 (1989), pp. 615-625.

32. Lynne N. Casper and Suzanne M. Bianchi, *Continuity and Change in the American Family* (Thousand Oaks, CA: Sage Publications, 2002), n.p.

33. Larry L. Bumpass, "National Survey of Families and Households, Working Papers," Nos. 2 and 5, collected by the Center for Demography and Ecology, University of Wisconsin, 1989.

34. Anonymous. http://members.aol.com/cohabiting/index.htm (accessed March 2002).

## Chapter 4

1. Wade Horn, "Fatherly Advice," *Washington Times*, March 31, 1998, n.p.

2. Nancy Fagan (Dr. Romance), "Commitment, Why Did He Leave Me?" http://www.committment.com/fagan5.html (accessed March 31, 2003).

3. Ibid.

## Chapter 6

1. Ann Landers, "Garth: The Moody Husband Won't Party On in Bedroom," *The Los Angeles Daily News*, March 20, 2002, p. 8.

2. Ibid.

3. 1 Samuel 18:1, *NASB* (emphasis added).

4. This concept is found in both negative and positive circumstances and is often translated as "conspired" (1 Sam. 22:8).

5. This is similar to how the half-completed wall that Nehemiah rebuilt was joined together in Jerusalem (see Neh. 4:6).

6. This is like tying a scroll of Scripture to a stone (see Jer. 51:63).

7. Putting Leviathan on a leash is something no one can do (see Job 41:5).

8. John 11:3,36.

9. Genesis 44:30.

10. See Genesis 44:31.

11. See Romans 12:10.

12. See Proverbs 17:17.

13. See Proverbs 18:24.

14. 1 Corinthians 13:4-8, *THE MESSAGE*.

15. See Ephesians 5:25,28-29,33; 1 Peter 3:7.

16. See Ephesians 5:22-33.
17. John 3:16.
18. 1 John 3:16.
19. See 1 John 4:7.
20. See Romans 5:5.
21. See Galatians 5:22-23.

## Chapter 7

1. Brian Gudgel, interview with author, August 1999, Agoura Hills, CA.
2. California Highway Patrol Officer, interview with author, September 1999, Woodland Hills, CA.
3. *National Highway Traffic Safety Administration.* http://www.nhtsha.dot.gov/people/injury/newdriver/safeteens/append (accessed January 4, 2003).
4. Genesis 2:25.
5. Hebrews 13:4, *THE MESSAGE.*
6. Proverbs 5:18-19, *THE MESSAGE.*
7. Song of Songs 7:7.
8. 1 Thessalonians 4:3, *THE MESSAGE.*
9. Ephesians 5:3, *THE MESSAGE.*
10. Hebrews 13:4, *THE MESSAGE.*
11. Romans 13:13, *THE MESSAGE.*
12. Genesis 2:24.
13. 1 Corinthians 6:13,18.
14. 1 Peter 2:11.
15. See 1 Corinthians 7:9.
16. 1 Thessalonians 4:3-4.
17. Curtis C. Mitchell, *Let's Live! Christ in Everyday Life* (Old Tappan, NJ: Fleming H. Revell, 1975), p. 54.
18. See 2 Timothy 2:22; 1 Corinthians 6:18.
19. Ephesians 5:18, *NLT.*
20. See Galatians 5:23.
21. Christopher Jencks, quoted in David Whitman, "The Trouble with Premarital Sex," *U.S. News and World Report* (May 19, 1997), p. 60.

## Chapter 8

1. Proverbs 11:14, *NASB.*
2. Proverbs 15:22, *NASB.*
3. Proverbs 24:6, *NASB.*
4. I recommend the Prepare/Enrich Program from Life Innovations, Inc., P.O. Box 190, Minneapolis, MN 55440-0190.

## Chapter 9

1. Psalm 127:1, *THE MESSAGE.*
2. Proverbs 24:3-4.
3. Matthew 7:24-27.
4. 1 Peter 2:4,6.
5. See John 14:16,18.
6. See Ephesians 1:19-20; 3:16,20.
7. See Galatians 5:22-23.
8. Nick Stinnett, *Secrets of Strong Families* (Boston: Little, Brown and Company, 1986), n.p.
9. James Dobson, *Love for a Lifetime* (Phoenix, AZ: Questar Publishers, 1987), n.p.
10. Billy Graham, "You Can Have a Better Home," *Decision Magazine* (February 1991), p. 3.

## Chapter 10

1. Genesis 2:24.
2. See Matthew 19:5; Mark 10:7; Ephesians 5:31.
3. Clifford Penner, *Getting Your Sex Life Off to a Great Start* (Waco, TX: Word Publishing, 1994), p. 70.
4. See Genesis 29:27.
5. David Whitman, "The Trouble with Premarital Sex: Do the Prudes Have a Point?" *U.S. News and World Report* (May 19, 1997), p. 56.
6. Barbara Freedman, "Woman Feels Betrayed by Boyfriend," *Ventura (California) Star,* August 27, 2000, p. E4.
7. Ibid.
8. Ibid.
9. *Webster's Revised Unabridged Dictionary,* 1913, s.v. "marriage."
10. *The Oxford English Dictionary,* 1933, s.v. "marriage."
11. *The American Heritage Dictionary,* 4th ed., s.v. "marriage."

## Chapter 11

1. Ruth W. Berenda, quoted in James Dobson, *Hide or Seek* (Old Tappan, NJ: Fleming H. Revell, 1974), pp. 116-117.
2. See 1 Peter 2:11.
3. Proverbs 4:23.
4. See 1 Timothy 1:19.
5. See 1 Timothy 4:2; 1 Corinthians 8:12; 1 Corinthians 8:7.
6. A. C. Green, quoted in "The Trouble with Premarital Sex: Do the Prudes Have a Point?" *U.S. News and World Report* (May 19, 1997), p. 59.

7. George Washington, quoted in Robert J. Ellis, "Laments Loss of Character," *Augusta (Georgia) Chronicle,* September 19, 1998, opinion page.

## Chapter 12

1. See John 4:1-42.
2. John 4:17-18, *NKJV*.
3. Laura Schlessinger, "Early Housewarming," *Los Angeles Daily News,* April 12, 1998, n.p.
4. Ibid.
5. See Matthew 1:19.
6. See Luke 1:28,42; Matthew 1:19.

## Chapter 13

1. Song of Songs 3:6-11.
2. Song of Songs 4:1-11.
3. Song of Songs 4:16.
4. Song of Songs 5:1.
5. Dannah Gresh, *And the Bride Wore White* (Chicago: Moody Press, 1999), p. 127.
6. Song of Songs 5:2.